Dedicated to those who stand for the Republic and its Laws:

Preet Bharara
James Clapper
James Comey
Loretta Lynch
Andrew McCabe
Sally Yates
Robert Mueller

Cover design by Nancy Randolph,
image by permission of Dave Granlund

USEFUL ASSETS

The Trump Family, the Russians and Eurasian Organized Crime

by

Robert C. Williams

Robt C Will (signature)

*For Bob + Abigail —
With best wishes
Bob* (handwritten inscription)

DORRANCE
PUBLISHING CO
EST. 1920
PITTSBURGH, PENNSYLVANIA 15238

Dorrance Publishing Co
585 Alpha Drive
Pittsburgh, PA 15238
Visit our website at www.dorrancebookstore.com

ISBN: 978-1-4809-8773-9
eISBN: 978-1-4809-8796-8

The Russians have succeeded, I believe,
beyond their wildest expectations.
James Clapper, former Director of National Intelligence,
October 2017, *Politico* interview

Trump signals a far more troubling mindset—
one in which the truth isn't so much absent or contested
as it doesn't matter. This is both deeply cynical and strangely
hopeful—a wish that maybe no one will notice.
Or not mind if they do. The truth is, he was right.
What Trump really heralds is a time when there
are no more experts.
Kevin Young, *Bunk. The Rise of Hoaxes, Humbug, Plagiarists,*
Phonies, Post-Facts, and Fake News (2017), 444-5.

CONTENTS

PREFACE

Trump's relationship with Russia goes back many, many years.
I'm sure the FBI has been monitoring it.
—Robert Amsterdam, attorney, April 2017

How did a bankrupt, friendless, and narcissistic New York real estate and casino mogul and womanizer escape bankruptcy and become elected U.S. President? Might he be criminally complicit in wire and mail fraud, money laundering, tax evasion, failing to register as a foreign agent, obstruction of justice, racketeering, conspiracy against the U.S., and even treason because of his longstanding dealings with agents of Vladimir Putin, Russia, and Russian (or Eurasian) organized crime? Is he a Russian asset, an FBI informant, or both? How has Eurasian capital flight through hidden offshore shell companies and banks helped Trump recover from his six bankruptcies without revealing his Eurasian sources? Has Trump historically escaped jail time by borrowing money from organized crime and the banks in order to settle cases out of court?

Current FBI, Congressional and special counsel investigations focus on the influence of the Russian government on the Trump presidential campaign of 2016 and possible obstruction of justice as president. But the story of Trump's links to Russian organized crime and the FBI through his real estate and casino operations begins well before 1987, when the Soviet KGB arranged Trump's first trip to Moscow, or even 1977 when he married a Czech.[1] This is a very old

---

[1] There are numerous Trump biographies, none of which explore his links to Russian and Eurasian organized crime in any detail. See especially: Wayne Barrett, *Trump, The Greatest Show on Earth. The Deals, the Downfall, the Reinvention*

story, and definitely not "fake news" limited to his presidential campaign. Trump's history involves many Russians (and Eurasians), with Trump having deniable contact with Russian government officials. These individuals were usually part of Vladimir Putin's family- and clan-based kleptocracy[2] but did not actually serve in the government, giving Putin plausible deniability about any involvement in their actions. One degree of separation insulates.

The term "useful idiot" (*poleznyi durak*) was used by Soviet intelligence after the 1930s purges for a naïve individual who could serve as an unwitting asset or agent. (U.S. Ambassador Joseph Davies swallowing and parroting Stalin's explanations of the Purges comes to mind.) The term "mafia state" is often used to describe Vladimir Putin's worldwide kleptocracy of wealthy thieves hiding their assets in offshore accounts, but in contact and collusion with the *ad hoc* Russian government. Both concepts may be applicable in looking at Trump's longstanding relationship with "Russian-based organized crime" (RBOC, or "Eurasian" organized crime) worldwide, with which Trump has long been a business partner, friend, and collaborator.

Both American and Eurasian mafias observed a code of silence and manliness (*Omerta*), loyalty to an extended family, abstinence in the liquor and drugs that made them wealthy, opposition to the authorities, and a fondness for revenge against anyone who might betray family loyalty and trust. The Trump family has a similar code, but they occupy the White House and have longstanding ties to Russian and Eurasian organized crime. No wonder Trump won the vote in Russian-dominated Brighton Beach, and nowhere else, in his home town of New York City in 2016.

(NY: Regan Arts, 1992); David Cay Johnson, *The Making of Donald Trump* (NY: Melville House, 2016); Kenneth F. McCallion, *The Essential Guide to Donald Trump* (NY: Bryant Park Press, 2016). The most recent account of Trump's link to the Russians is by *Guardian* journalist Luke Harding, *Collusion. Secret Meetings, Dirty Money, and how Russia helped Donald Trump Win* (NY: Vintage Books, 2017).

[2] Karen Dawisha, *Putin's Kleptocracy. Who Owns Russia?* (NY: Simon & Schuster, 2014). Kleptocracy is the rule of thieves.

USEFUL ASSETS

Abbreviations:

APT = Advanced Persistent Threat

CA= Cambridge Analytica

CAATSA= Countering America's Adversaries through Sanctions Act (2017)

CIA= Central Intelligence Agency (1948)

DNC= Democratic National Committee

DNI= Director of National Intelligence

EDNY= Eastern District of New York

FARA= Foreign Agent Registration Act (1938)

FBI= Federal Bureau of Investigation

FISA= Foreign Intelligence Surveillance Act (1978)

FSB= Federal Security Service (*Federal'nyi sluzhba bezopastnosti*) [Russia]

GRU= Russian/Soviet military intelligence

IRA= Internet Research Agency

KGB= Committee on State Security (Soviet police)

NRA= National Rifle Association

NSA= National Security Agency

NSC= National Security Council

RICO= Racketeer Influenced and Corrupt Organizations Act (1970)

RBOC= Russian Based Organized Crime

SDNY= Southern District of New York

STB= State Security Service (Czech)

ACKNOWLEDGMENTS

Charles Dunbar; Clare Durst; Jack Henderson;
Seymour Hersh; George Hudson; Mark Kramer; Victor
Papacosma; Russell Pierce; Ann Williams; Peter Williams.

INTRODUCTION:

FROM "INTEGRITY" TO "TRUMP" AT MAR-A-LAGO

Davies and Trump Heraldry for Mar- a-Lago (NY Times)

In 1939, the British government awarded Joseph E. Davies, the retiring U.S. ambassador to Moscow (whose ancestry was Welsh), a heraldic coat of arms with three lions on a shield and the name *"Integritas"* on a banner below. The Davies coat of arms promptly emerged as a symbol for his Miami estate, *Mar-a-Lago* (Lake by the Sea), owned by Davies' second wife, Marjorie Merriweather Post, after her divorce from wealthy financier E.F. Hutton, who built Mar-a-Lago between 1925 and 1927. Marjorie selected the land parcel, and the Hutton's 55,000-square foot mansion contained 118 rooms. After World War II, she dreamed of giving Mar-a-Lago to the American people as a winter White House for future presidents. Ultimately, she did so.

Marjorie Post was a socialite Russophile and an avid collector of Russian decorative art, most of which she acquired in Moscow commission stores during her husband's ambassadorship (1935-1939) at the height of Joseph Stalin's paranoid and violent purges featuring fake show trials of conspirators.[3] Post housed her Russian art collection (including several valuable Faberge Imperial eggs) in Hillwood, her Washington D.C. mansion in Rock Creek Park. She also entertained numerous Russ-ian visitors at Mar-a-Lago, notably during the 1929 Florida visit of Grand Duke Alexander Mikhailovich, a cousin of Nicholas II, whose son Nikita was one of several claimants to the nonexistent Imperial Russian throne.

Stalin and his agents considered Davies to be a "useful idiot." He knew virtually nothing about the Soviet Union, the Russian lan-guage, or the violent history of the revolution now unfolding with the collectivization of the peasantry, forced industrialization, and the purge of "enemies of the people." Yet Davies attended the meticu-lously choreographed show trials in Moscow and became convinced of a vast conspiracy of class traitors and enemies plotting against the benevolent Stalin. Davies often swallowed Soviet propaganda whole. He was a useful, if unwitting, asset because he was a well-placed Washington attorney who played poker weekly with U.S. President Franklin D. Roosevelt and a few close friends. For the Soviet leaders in Moscow, Davies was a friend, asset, and useful idiot at court in Washington D.C. But not an agent.

Mar-a-Lago languished during and after World War II. The Davies' were rarely in residence, and the upkeep was expensive, even for a millionaire heiress to the C.W. Post cereal fortune. Marjorie di-vorced Joe Davies in 1964 (her fourth divorce), remarried briefly, and died in 1973, bequeathing her mansion to the U.S. Department of the Interior as a presidential retreat. (Presidents Nixon, Ford, Carter, and Reagan had no interest.) But Mar-a-Lago turned out to be a White Elephant and the government returned it to the Post Founda-tion rather than pay millions of dollars annually for its maintenance. In 1980, Mar-a-Lago was declared a National Historic Landmark. It was also a national budget sinkhole.

---

[3] On Post, Davies, and their collecting of Russian art objects during the Stalinist purges, see Robert C. Williams, *Russian Art and American Money, 1900-1940* (Cambridge MA: Harvard University Press, 1980), 229-262.

Flamboyant New York realtor and womanizer Donald J. Trump purchased Mar-a-Lago for a relative song ($9 million) in 1985 with bank mortgage loans and a minimal personal down payment. After a long battle with the city of Palm Beach, he opened the estate to the public as the Mar-a-Lago Club. Annual membership fees climbed to $100,000 annually, doubling after Trump became U.S. president.

Trump stole the coat of arms from the Davies family for himself. Instead of "integrity," the banner now read "Trump." In 2007, Trump tried to use his pirated coat of arms for his hotels and golf clubs in the U.K., but sharp-eyed British heraldry keepers noted the similarity with the Davies coat of arms and refused to register Trump's stolen symbolism. Then they banned it. Members of the Davies family threatened to sue Trump but were warned off by one of the Davies' grandsons, U.S. Senator Joseph Tydings of Maryland (who visited Mar-a-Lago often as a child). Trump would simply gain publicity from any lawsuit, which was likely to go on for years. As a result, Trump continued to use his coat of arms at Mar-a-Lago and his numerous U.S. golf clubs. In 2010, Trump registered a U.S. trademark for a heraldic coat of arms containing the wording "Trump" in gold. But his fake insignia is banned in Britain.

Unwittingly, Donald Trump, by purchasing Mar- a-Lago, acquired an inheritance of Russian art collecting, Soviet history, and the family property of a leading U.S. politician and ambassador with deep ties to the New Deal that Trump would ultimately try to dismantle. The Davies' were pro-Russian, pro-Soviet, and deferential to Russian dictators. So was Trump. From the points of view of Stalin and Putin, they were all "useful idiots," dispensing propaganda in the West as part of a Soviet disinformation campaign without having the slightest idea they were doing so. They were *assets*, but too incompetent and uncontrollable to be *agents*.

ASSETS

Donald and Ivana Zelnickova Trump in Leningrad, 1987.
(Maxim Blokhin, TASS)

1. IVANA ZELNICKOVA, CZECH MATE

Ironically, the anti-immigrant Donald J. Trump, whose mother was a Scot and father a German-American, married a Czech immigrant. Czech intelligence, and consequently the Soviet KGB (later the Russian FSB), spied on Trump and his family ever since Trump in 1977 acquired a bride who was a citizen of a communist country. As was

1

typical during the Cold War, the FBI and CIA, two mutually unco-operative U.S. federal agencies, undoubtedly conducted their own ob-servations of the highly publicized and self-advertising Trump family.

Czech intelligence had long used women as "honey traps" or "swallows." In 1961, a Czech prostitute named *Mariella Novotny*, age 20, gained notoriety because of her work as a striptease dancer in New York and Washington, where she became one of JFK's many sexual partners.[4] Arrested by the FBI and charged with soliciting, Novotny returned to London and became involved with Soviet agents in the so-called Profumo Affair. After John Profumo resigned as British Sec-retary of State for War in June 1963, Novotny maintained her lavish lifestyle through the generosity of her much older British husband, Horace Dibben. She died of a drug overdose in 1983.

In the wake of the 1968 Prague Spring, Soviet and Warsaw Pact troops invaded communist Czechoslovakia to suppress a liberal-na-tionalist armed rebellion that threatened both the Communist regime and the unity of the Soviet bloc. Many Czechs and Slovaks fled their native land and sought refuge in Europe and the U.S. Czech intelli-gence consequently became more active in the U.S., bringing agents into the country through Canada. Czech agents usually obtained a Canadian passport and developed a personal "legend" before entering the U.S. from Toronto or Montreal.

In March 1969, a Czech historian of Russia, *Thomas Riha*, dis-appeared from his house in Boulder, Colorado. Riha's body has never been found. Companion *Galya Tannenbaum*, a convicted forger known as "The Colonel," was imprisoned for forgery and for her in-volvement in several cyanide poisoning cases. She introduced Riha to his young Czech wife, *Hana Hruska*, 24. The Riha marriage lasted only four months. Intelligence officers of several countries disavowed any involvement with Riha, but he served in U.S. army intelligence during the Korean War and studied in Moscow just before Lee Har-vey Oswald arrived there in October 1959. The Riha case drove a wedge between the FBI and CIA over jurisdictional issues. As a result,

---

[4] On Mariella Novotny and the Profumo Affair, see Christine Keeler, *The Truth at Last. My Story*. (London: Sidgwick & Jackson, 2001), 194, 270-1.

the two agencies stopped sharing information for several years. Both naturally denied Riha was ever their own agent.[5]

The most damaging Czech spy in the U.S. was *Karl Koecher*, a "false defector" who arrived in 1965 specifically trained by Czech intelligence to join the CIA.[6] After six years of graduate study at Indiana and Columbia universities, Koecher worked for the CIA from 1973 until his arrest in 1984. He and his wife Hana led a "swinging" life with other couples and maintained her cover as a diamond merchant in Manhattan. They were ultimately exchanged at the Berlin "bridge of spies" for a famous Russian dissident, Natan Sharansky, and others, in 1986, and then permanently expelled from the U.S.

Koecher was at the time the only foreign agent ever to penetrate the CIA. His damage to U.S. agents at home and abroad was incalculable (and classified). He was clearly the most important Czech spy in the U.S. during the Cold War, when stories of legends, dead drops, moles, double agents, disappearances, murder and "honey traps" were the stuff of spy novels as well as reality.

Target Trump

Ivana Zelnickova, Trump's first wife, was a Czech citizen.[7] In 1971, Zelnickova's boyfriend, Czech skier *George Syrovatka*, arranged her "green card" marriage to *Alfred Winkelmayr*, an Austrian friend, so that Ivana could obtain a western passport. Despite her "Cold War marriage," Ivana remained in Prague and studied at Charles University. Then, in 1973, Ivana followed Syrovatka to Montreal and lived with him until 1976, using a Canadian passport, although there is no record of any marriage. Zelnickova then met her future husband Donald J. Trump. In her fractured English, Ivana called him "The Donald" and the nickname stuck.

---

[5] On the Thomas Riha case and its detrimental impact on CIA-FBI relations, see Mark Riebling, *Wedge. The Secret War between the FBI and CIA* (NY: Alfred A. Knopf, 1994), 251-6.

[6] On the Koechers, see Ron Kessler, *Spy vs. Spy. Stalking Soviet Spies in America* (London: David and Charles, 1988), and *The Secrets of the FBI* (NY: Random House, 2011), 73-7.

[7] On Ivana Zelnickova Trump in Canada, see Barrett, *Trump* 128-32.

Czech intelligence (STB, or state secret security), working with and directly under the Soviet KGB, began tracking Donald J. Trump by 1977, when he married (on April 9 in a wedding ceremony officiated by Norman Vincent Peale) Ivana, 28, a Czech model born in Zlin, a shoe and aircraft manufacturing center in Moravia. Zelnickova also had a job pumping gas and an alleged tour on a Czech national (not Olympic) ski team. She lived in Montreal with Syrovatka, after her first marriage to Winkelmayr and helped run Syrovatka's ski boutique. By then, the Czechs had opened a file on Ivana, and on her father Milos, a Czech engineer, to which they added material on her new family in Manhattan, the Trumps, after their marriage. Thus, the Czechs, the Soviet KGB, and the Russian FSB have been tracking the Trumps since at least 1977. Perhaps Trump could someday become a "useful idiot." Or better yet, an asset or agent subject to blackmail.

Trump was well known as a wealthy and colorful New York real estate mogul and womanizer. His personal wealth and his real estate companies were mainly an inheritance from his father, Fred Trump, a Queens realtor and Ku Klux Klan sympathizer (arrested in 1927 for participating in a Klan demonstration) who refused to rent to African-Americans. (The Department of Justice filed a civil rights lawsuit against the Trumps for violating the 1969 Fair Housing Act, a suit later settled.) Trump's grandfather, Friedrich Trumpf, had emigrated from Germany in 1885, become a naturalized citizen in 1892, and made his fortune in Seattle and the Yukon off alcohol, prostitution, and gambling. Yet despite prolonged prenuptial negotiations with Ivana, lawyers were unable to calculate Trump's financial net worth because his holdings, shell companies, and bank accounts were so widely distributed under so many different names. Trump's unknown wealth largely lay hidden in offshore accounts and was disguised by numerous bank loans. It still is. Donald Trump was never as wealthy as he seemed.

Cold War espionage was intense. On October 3, 1984, the FBI office in New York arrested *Alice Michelson*, 67, an East German spy headed for Czechoslovakia, at JFK airport. Sentenced to 10 years in prison, Michelson was immediately exchanged for U.S. spies in the

Soviet Union. Another Cold War marriage that attracted both the FBI and Czech intelligence was one in 1979 between hedge-fund tycoon and Trump friend *Carl Icahn*, who married Czech ballerina *Liba Treibal* in New York City that year. Icahn later became Trump's White House consultant, having liquidated the insolvent Trump Taj Mahal in Atlantic City for Trump. Icahn also engineered a hostile takeover of TWA airlines in 1985.

At the same time, General *V. A. Kryuchkov*, head of the KGB's First Chief Directorate, responsible for acquiring foreign intelligence, was anxious to improve agent recruitment in the U.S. and Europe. Good collaborators and contacts seemed in short supply. Yet two of them—Aldrich Ames at the CIA and Robert Hanssen at the FBI— would become famously effective moles and spies burrowed for years within U.S. intelligence and law enforcement agencies.

In August 1985, Soviet KGB officer *Vladimir Putin*, 33, was posted to Dresden, East Germany, where he lived frugally with his wife and two children until returning to Leningrad in 1990. Putin was assigned to Directorate S, the illegal intelligence-gathering unit of the KGB, working with the East German Stasi to prepare foreign agents with forged papers and false identities. One of his Stasi colleagues was *Matthias Warnig*, now on the council of Putin's VTB bank in Moscow and managing director of Nord Stream AG, which operates the natural gas pipeline between Russia and Germany. The Stasi awarded Putin a bronze medal in 1988 for his services. The "illegals" were agents who kept their affiliation with the Soviet state and the communist party a secret. Putin recruited Soviet agents at American military bases in West Germany, and certainly knew of other agents in Europe and the U.S.[8]

Dresden was the closest German city to Prague, but we have no record of a Putin visit there at the time. Yet it is difficult to imagine that Putin did not have knowledge of the KGB and Czech files on the

---

[8] Little is known about Putin's years as a young KGB officer in Dresden. See Masha Gessen, *The Man without a Face. The Unlikely Rise of Vladimir Putin* (NY: Penguin, 2014); Stephen Myers, *The New Tsar. The Rise and Reign of Vladimir Putin* (NY: Vintage, 2016); Richard Lourie, *Putin. His Downfall and Russia's Coming Crash* (NY: St. Martin's Press, 2017), 39-48.

Trumps and their well publicized life in New York. Or that he did not visit Prague on occasion.

By the time the Trumps divorced in 1992, the Czech "cover" on the family included periodic wiretaps on their telephones, surveillance by Czech agents with code names like *Lubos* and *Al Jarza*, and opening and reading the postal traffic between Zlin and New York. Agents reported that Trump's businesses were "absolutely safe," and "he is completely tax-exempt for the next 30 years." They also speculated that Trump might well run for U.S. president in 1992 or 1996. He did not.

Czech agents likewise reported on a cooperative delegation from Slusovice, where Ivana's father lived, that visited New York in late 1989, on the summer visits of Ivana and Donald Trump Jr. to see her father in Czechoslovakia, and on Milos' visits to see his daughter's family in the U.S. Czech agents also tapped Milos's telephone and opened his mail.

Recently opened Czech files indicate that the KGB had a substantial dossier on the Trumps by the time Donald and Ivana made their first trip to Russia in July 1987.[9] The new Soviet ambassador in Washington, *Yury Dubinin*, had visited New York in March 1986 as Soviet representative to the U.N. and was (according to his daughter) eager to recruit, or hook, Trump in some way. Trump and Dubinin met first in Trump Tower, then at a luncheon in New York that autumn. In January 1987, Dubinin wrote Trump a letter inviting him to Moscow, all expenses paid, as a guest of the Soviet government. He dangled the possibility of a new Trump Tower in Moscow. The Trumps stayed at the National Hotel near Red Square that July with Ivana's assistant, Lisa Calandra. Kryuchkov, naturally had the hotel rooms bugged in search of *kompromat*, compromising material that might facilitate blackmailing these young Americans with money and flattery into a useful relationship with the KGB. Trump wanted a Russian deal to help make himself rich; Kryuchkov wanted another useful idiot and asset in America.

By late 1987, the American press was speculating that Donald J.

---

[9] On Kryuchkov, the KGB and the Trump visit of 1987, see Harding, *Collusion*, 215-30.

Trump might just run for U.S. president. Thirty years later, he did. The Soviets had meddled in U.S. elections with "active measures" before: in 1948 against Harry S Truman; in 1964 against Barry Goldwater; in 1968 with a failed bribe attempt directed at Hubert Humphrey; in 1984 versus Ronald Reagan. American election meddling abroad was equally well established after World War II in Europe, Asia, and Latin America. In KGB eyes, the Trumps were certainly worth cultivating as a possible future asset. As a trained professional agent, Trump was a laughable prospect, unpredictable and uncontrollable. But his contacts and money made him a potential asset.

In 1988, Ivana Trump became a naturalized U.S. citizen. Her father *Milos Zelnickov* died in 1990, and she attended his funeral service in Zlin with the Trump family in tow. In 1993, after the Trumps divorced, so did Slovakia and the Czech Republic. And when Trump visited Moscow again in 1996, Russia's leading administrator of gambling casinos met Trump and guessed he might well be a future American president. His guess was correct.

Prague and Eurasian Organized Crime

Czechoslovakia was also becoming a center of a worldwide network of Russian and Eurasian organized crime, a significant part of the Soviet black-market economy. In 1990, Russia's most powerful mobster, *Semion Mogilevich*, left Moscow and began to establish organized crime networks worldwide.[10] Brutal enforcers, hitmen, and torturers were based in villas in Ricany, near Prague. Mogilevich soon began smuggling heroin and cocaine into Russia from the U.S. and Canada. He married Hungarian Katalin Papp in 1991 and set up his headquarters in Budapest. Activities of Mogilevich's criminal empire soon involved casinos, arms deals, drugs, money laundering, and prostitution.

Russian president *Boris Yeltsin* visited Prague in 1993, admitting during the visit that the 1968 Soviet invasion of Czechoslovakia had

---

[10] On Semion Mogilevich and Russian/Eurasian organized crime, see the FBI's 1998 report "Semion Mogilevich Organization, Eurasian Organized Crime," Department of Justice, Washington DC, August 1998. See also Misha Glenny, *McMafia. A Journal through the Global Criminal Underworld* (NY: Random House, 2008), 71-96.

been an act of aggression. The Czech Republic and Slovakia became separate nations after the collapse of the Soviet Union, then NATO members. The enterprising Mogilevich quickly set up a jewelry business in Moscow and Budapest to fence stolen art and antiques as valuable assets began to leave Russia for the West. By the time Putin became aware of his organized crime network in 1990s St. Petersburg, Mogilevich ran a vast empire of illegal business at home and abroad.

The Soviet collapse in 1991 bred crime and violence. Putin was horrified at the Soviet collapse. His position in the mayor's office in St. Petersburg involved him with gangsters who threatened his family. His contract with his friend *Gennady Timchenko* angered many in the local organized crime network. (Timchenko later sponsored Putin's judo club.) And he came to know Semion Mogilevich as well as Putin's future supporter *Igor Sechin*, head of Rosneft, the state energy company.

On May 31, 1995, Czech police stormed the summit meeting of Eurasian mob leaders at the U Holubu restaurant in Prague, owned by Mogilevich and used as a money-laundering center. Czech police arrested, detained, and fingerprinted some 200 mobsters. Five attendees (including Mogilevich) were declared *persona non grata* by the Czech Republic government. Mogilevich was banned from the Czech Republic for a decade. He also appeared on the FBI's "most wanted" list, where he remained for many years.

Meanwhile, FBI director *Louis Freeh* announced the creation of a new FBI office in Moscow to deal with Russian and Eurasian organized crime. The office opened in July 1994 with two full-time FBI agents in cooperation with the new Russian government of *Boris Yeltsin*. Putin continued his work in St. Petersburg by arranging contracts with foreign businessmen through the mayor's office.

After succeeding Yeltsin as Russian president, Putin visited Prague in 2006. Eight years later, in 2014, Czech Republic president *Milos Zeman* invited Putin to visit the city again. In the meantime, Putin had involved Russia with military conflicts in Chechnia, Georgia, Crimea, and Ukraine.

With Donald Trump's surprise election as U.S. president in 2016, Ivana Trump (by then his first of three wives, and long divorced from

Trump) announced, perhaps jokingly, that she would like to be the U.S. ambassador to Prague in the near future. In December 2016, Trump invited President Zeman, who shared Trump's anti-immigration, pro-Russian, and anti-Muslim biases, to visit the White House in April 2017. He did not visit, but was handily reelected by the Czechs as president in January 2018.

In December 2015, U.S. General *Michael Flynn* showed up in Moscow for an all-expenses paid trip to celebrate the tenth anniversary of *Russia Today*, Putin's English-language propaganda TV station. *Russia Today* was founded in 2005 by *Mikhail Lesin*, Yeltsin's and then Putin's press agent, recently murdered in Washington DC on November 5, 2015, just before testifying on his publication to the U.S. Department of Justice. Seated at Putin's table at dinner, Flynn must have been surprised to find *Cyril Swoboda*, the former deputy prime minister, foreign minister, and interior minister of the Czech Republic, a man once in charge of the STB and Czech intelligence. Who picked up the Czech? And why? Did the Czechs arrange a secret meeting of Trump attorney Michael Cohen in Prague with Russians shortly before the American election?

In any event, Putin was clearly plotting a strategy of interference in the coming presidential elections in the United States. Perhaps that was why *Jill Stein*, a candidate, was at the table.

Moscow, December 2015: Who picked up the Czech?

In March 2017, U.S. NATO troops and armored vehicles were welcomed in a Prague parade demonstrating U.S. and NATO (Czechs are now NATO members) commitment to national independence in the face of Russian aggression. In April, Milos Zeman announced he expected visits from the Chinese president in May and from Russian president, Putin, in November, suggesting that Trump might wish to join a peace conference in Prague at some later date.

Donald Trump has longstanding links to Eastern Europe through his Czech ex-wife. As they raised their three children during the 1980s, and he consummated extensive real estate and casino deals in New York. Those links extended to Russian and Eurasian organized crime as well. Trump involved his wife, two sons, and a daughter (and son-in-law) in many of his business enterprises. Wealthy Russians sought to invest their capital in London and New York real estate, including Trump buildings. They gambled in Trump casinos in Atlantic City, stayed at Trump hotels in New York, Miami, and Las Vegas. The Trump brand thus became an extended family affair linked to Russia, the Soviet Union, and Eastern Europe through international finance and organized crime. Trump hotels were safe havens.

Anti-Trump Demonstrators outside Trump Tower
after the November 2016 presidential election.

2. TRUMP TOWER, THE RUSSIA HOUSE

Trump's life intertwines with the underworld.
—Wayne Barrett, *The Greatest Show on Earth* (1993)

I believe on occasion I used that name.
—Donald Trump, under oath
about his fake identity, "John Barron" (1990)

In the 1980s, Trump Tower in New York (at 721 Fifth Avenue) became a new kind of center for Eurasian organized crime, gambling and foreign investment operating under the nose of the FBI, often without the Bureau's knowledge.

Russian emigres had long played a key role in the New York underworld. During the 1970s, Russian organized crime developed networks among the Odessa (and other) mafias or gangs forming in the Brighton Beach and Crown Heights sections of Brooklyn. Thousands of Soviet refugees emigrated to the U.S. in the seventies. Many were Jewish. The Russian mafiosi soon exceeded the Sicilian Cosa Nostra families in their murderous activities. Those with sufficient funds begin to acquire valuable real estate in the New York area. They included Russians, Ukrainians, Kazakhs, and other "Eurasians" seeking to export and invest the money and capital they had somehow obtained from the old USSR. Trump Tower became one of their headquarters, a casino and safe haven for Eurasian organized crime.

In 1973, Donald J. Trump met *Roy Cohn*, the ruthless boy-wonder prosecuting attorney made famous by the 1951 Rosenberg atomic spy trial, the McCarthy-era witch-hunting, and the "un-American activity" hearings in Washington D.C. Cohn was a smart, savvy, sleazy tax cheat who demanded absolute loyalty and dished out innuendo, conspiracy, lies, and accusations in pursuit of profit and revenge for his clients, many of them criminals and mobsters.[11] Cohn taught his protégé Donald Trump to never surrender, always attack your accuser,

---

[11] On Roy Cohn, see Nicholas Hoffman, *Citizen Cohn. The Life and Times of Roy Cohn* (NY: Doubleday,1998). Also, see Johnston, *Trump*, 33-47.

lie about everything and call your accusers liars themselves, claim victory, and never admit defeat or apologize. One should lie constantly, advised Cohn, and always blame others for your mistakes. Admit nothing, and blame everyone else. Like Joseph Goebbels, Cohn was a master of the Big Lie, endlessly repeated. Trump lamented Cohn's absence after he was gone.

"Where is my Roy Cohn?" Trump recently complained, confusing his personal attorney with the attorney general of the U.S.

Red-baiting Senator Joseph McCarthy and his attorney, Roy Cohn, at the Army-McCarthy hearings in 1954.

In 1979, Trump, by now a colorful and self-promoting New York realtor, was the target of a *bribery* investigation. Trump hired Teamster labor organizer *Daniel Sullivan* (6'5", 300 pounds) to deal with Polish workers getting sub-par $4/hour salaries for demolishing the old Bon-Wit Teller store on the site of his projected Trump Tower. Most Poles were underpaid (or unpaid) and undocumented immigrants in need of work. They worked with electrical lines and asbestos without hard hats. Contractor *William Kaszyski*—not Trump—was convicted of importing and exploiting illegal Polish immigrants for the "Polish Brigade," sentenced to several months in jail, and fined $10,000. Trump escaped justice, having destroyed two valuable bas-reliefs on the building façade and been widely criticized by the media and the art world.

In October 1980, the New York Planning Commission voted to support Trump's $100 million plan to demolish the Bon-Wit Teller building and construct Trump Tower. His partner that financed construction was the Equitable Life Insurance Company. Trump's attack-dog attorney Roy Cohn won the tax abatement case in court on appeal. Construction soon began.

Meanwhile *Robert Hanssen*, 35, an FBI agent and Soviet military intelligence spy (GRU), moved to join the New York FBI office in 1979. Hanssen became expert on FBI wiretaps and began to provide information to the GRU. FBI eavesdropping—code-named POCKETWATCH—was based just north of Grand Central Terminal and focused on Aeroflot, Amtorg, and other Soviet agencies operating in Manhattan. The larger operation, MEGAHUT, tapped telephone lines throughout the city. Until 1986, Hanssen had access to all FBI wiretaps in the city and duly reported anything of interest to both the KGB and GRU.[12]

In 1980, Trump hired *Paul Manafort*, a Washington DC attorney in a lobbying partnership with *Roger Stone*, to serve as Trump's lawyer for gambling and real estate issues. He also got advice from Stone, who by 1988 was a very close confidante of Trump. Stone was half-Italian, half-Hungarian, and a baptized Catholic who provided a link between the Cosa Nostra and Ukrainian mobster Semion Mogilevich. He allegedly sported a tattoo of Richard Nixon on his backside. Stone was also Cohn's contact with Ronald Reagan and the White House in the 1980s.

Trump also began his lifelong use of fake identities to spread rumors, denials, and fake news among the press and public. (His father Fred often made disinformation telephone calls as "Mr. Green.") In dealing with press criticism of the Polish Brigade and the destroyed bas reliefs, Trump made phone calls as "John Barron," a pseudonym he used throughout the 1980s.[13] John Barron was in fact a well-known

---

[12] Robert Hanssen was a Soviet spy who worked for both the CIA and FBI. His FBI duties in the 1980s included wiretapping the United Nations and other prominent buildings housing Soviet citizens. See David Wise, *The Inside Story of how the FBI's Robert Hanssen betrayed America* (NY: Random House, 2002).

[13] On "John Barron" and other Trump fake identities, see Barrett, *Trump*, 304 and Johnston, *Trump*, 74-5, 135-8, 148-52. The real John Barron in 1974 authored

Reader's Digest investigative reporter who had published popular books on the Soviet KGB (1974, revised 1985), Chappaquiddick, and FBI informant Morris Childs, a CPUSA courier to and from Moscow. Cartoons in 2017 had Trump naming "John Barron" as his new FBI director. The real John Barron died in 2005. But the pseudonym lives on in Trump's youngest son, Barron, who wears a mocking t-shirt that proclaims "expert."

In 1981, the FBI subpoenaed Trump in a NYC *racketeering* probe, asking Trump about Teamster leader John Cody and the Gambino crime family. Trump employee Daniel Sullivan had dealt with the Polish Brigade. One day in April, two FBI agents visited Trump at his offices with Sullivan, who was also an FBI informer (he died in 1993). One of the agents was *Walter B. Stowe*, Sullivan's FBI handler, described later by Trump as a "high quality guy," but "not a pal". Stowe, 32, received his B.A. and J.D. from the College of William and Mary in Virginia and worked for the FBI from 1975 to 2001. After working as the FBI's Congressional Liaison, Stowe moved to Las Vegas in 2006 and worked for VendingData Corp. on legal compliance in the gaming industry.

The second FBI agent visiting Trump was *Damon Taylor*, 35, an organized crime expert who had served in Vietnam as a green beret and won the Bronze Star. Taylor worked in the FBI C-35 squad in NYC for three decades and was known as a man of honor and integrity before retiring as a security consultant.

The FBI hired *Sullivan* as an *informant*, code-name NY18904. According to Damon Taylor's FBI report[14], Trump told agents in June 1981 he wanted to "fully cooperate" with the FBI on his casino plans for mobbed-up Atlantic City, New Jersey, on land co-owned by Sullivan. Trump also suggested the FBI "use undercover Agents within the casino." By telling the N.J. Gaming Commission that Sullivan was his employee, Trump compromised the FBI investigation into

---

KGB. The Secret Work of Soviet Secret Agents (NY: Readers' Digest Press, 1974). There is no evidence Trump ever read Barron's book.

[14] Damon Taylor to Daniel Sullivan (NY18904-0) in FBI file SAC (137-22152), 9/22/1981. On Sullivan, see Barrett, *Trump*, 206-8, 219-22.

other casinos. Trump was thus "criminally compliant" with *obstruction of justice* charges, but was never charged. His FBI cooperation may well have saved him from a lawsuit and indictment.

FBI informants might be confidential (CI) and never testify in court. CIs could be "high level," "long term" (over six years), or "privileged." They might receive cash payments or nothing at all for their information. Or they might be confidential witnesses (CW), who agree to testify if needed. Or they might be simply "sources of information."

At about this time, Robert Hanssen, the zealous Soviet mole in the FBI who was engaged in wiretapping operations in Manhattan (possibly including Trump Tower), was reassigned to the FBI head-quarters in Washington D.C., ironically in the old post office building that is now a Trump hotel.

Trump seemed to flourish. By 1983, Trump Tower was completed at a cost of $201 million in bank loans to Trump. Mafia crime families controlled the concrete and construction trades in New York, includ-ing building supplies and unions. Trump worked with S&A Concrete, owned by *Anthony "Fat Tony" Salerno* of the Gambino family, and Paul Castellano, the Gambino family don. Trump Tower utilized an enor-mous amount of concrete and a minimum of steel reinforcing rods. Sullivan negotiated with the Housewreckers Union for labor. Trump dealt with union boss *John Cody* through the Trump family's attorney *Roy Cohn*, whose clients included Thomas and Joseph Gambino, Tony Salerno, and other mobsters.[15]

After the completion of Trump Tower, the Housewreckers Union sued Trump for fraud (for $1 million) for knowingly em-ploying more than 150 undocumented "Polish Brigade" workers in demolition and construction. Many workers were never paid for their work at all. The Housewreckers Union pension funds were thus deprived of a source of income, so the Union sued Trump. The case was settled only in 1999 for an undisclosed amount of money

---

[15] On mob life in New York, see Joseph Bonano, *A Man of Honor*. (NY: Simon & Schuster, 1983).

17

(probably \$4 million), undoubtedly borrowed.[16] Illegal immigrants helped build Trump Tower. Trump paid them badly, if at all.

Anthony "Fat Tony" Salerno, who handled the Trump Tower concrete business for Donald J. Trump. Arrest photo from 1986.

On Valentine's Day 1983, Trump Tower officially held its Grand Opening with Trump's parents and Roy Cohn among the guests of honor. The Russian and Eurasian criminals had already become tenants and soon attracted the attention of the FBI. Tony Salerno's 1988 indictment listed his 8-million-dollar contract for concrete with Trump Plaza, another project. Salerno died in prison shortly thereafter.

David Bogatin, Tax Evader

By 1984, FBI wiretaps on resident Russian mafia tenants of Trump Tower were beginning to function. For example, *David Bogatin*, a gasoline bootlegger and tax evader, purchased five condos on Floor 53 of Trump Tower for \$6 million from Donald Trump personally. (Trump attended the Bogatin closing and met him there in person to sign papers.)[17] Bogatin worked with Columbo family capo *Michael Franzese*. He served in the Soviet army as an artillery officer in North Vietnam and was also a member of the Mogilevich "family." Bogatin

---

[16] On the Polish workers, see H.B. Glushakow, *'Mafia Don'. Donald Trump's 40 Years of Mob Ties* (NY: CreateSpace, 2016).

[17] On David Bogatin and Trump, see Barrett, *Trump* 194.

sold his Trump Tower mortgages to a member of the Genovese crime family using a mafia-controlled bank in Manhattan's Chelsea district. Bogatin then moved to Vienna and set up commercial banks in Poland to launder Russian monies moving out of the USSR.

David Bogatin, Trump Tower resident. (National Post)

On August 1, 1985, David Bogatin received a three-year prison sentence for *tax evasion* and *Motor Fuel Tax felony* in Albany, New York. He pled guilty and agreed to pay $5 million in back taxes. He then skipped bail and fled to Poland. The State of New York seized Bogatin's Trump Tower apartments. Prosecutors concluded that Bogatin used the apartments to launder money, to shelter and hide assets, and for private parties.

Robert Hanssen returned to the FBI office in Manhattan from DC. He now offered his services (for money) to the KGB, not the GRU. His spy efforts shifted from wiretapping to identifying Soviet intelligence agents.

In 1986, mobster Tony Salerno was indicted, and legal charges mentioned Trump Plaza. Trump was also involved with a Bulgari jewelry store "empty box scam" to avoid paying the sales tax on $65,000 in purchases. Once again, Trump was criminally compliant, but not charged, in this instance with *tax evasion.*

Trump sold two 59th-floor condo units in Trump Tower to mobster *Robert Hopkins*, Luchese family boss and head of the largest *gambling* ring in New York. Hopkins was subsequently convicted of running over 100 gambling operations out of Trump Tower and arrested in his suite for murdering a rival gambler. (The charges were later dropped.)[18]

In July 1987, as we have seen, Trump and his Czech wife Ivana visited Moscow at Soviet expense looking for Trump hotel deals and stayed in the Lenin Suite of the National Hotel. But Russian hotel and casino projects failed to materialize, and Trump was unable to purchase any land for development that he would legally own. His first attempt to do business in Russia failed. And his attempt to build a casino in Australia also failed when the New South Wales police board, having listened to FBI transcripts of Trump phone conversations with Tony Salerno, warned against granting a license because of "Trump Mafia connections."[19]

After eight years abroad, in 1993, Poland extradited David Bogatin back to the U.S. for prison on various charges. As a result, Bogatin was jailed at Attica Prison in upstate New York for eight years.

Vadim Trincher, Racketeer and Illegal Gambler

In 1989, well known criminal *Vadim Trincher*, 30, emigrated to the U.S. from Kiev and began laundering money and sending it from Russia and Ukraine into U.S. via the *Bank of Cyprus.* Trincher later became a dual U.S.-Israeli citizen and lived in Trump Tower with his wife Elena and their two sons.

The collapse of the former Soviet Union led to the birth of the Russian Republic and the new "stans" in what Russians called the "near abroad." Thousands of former Soviet citizens emigrated to the

---

[18] Glushakow, *'Mafia' Don*, 47.

[19] Glushakow, *'Mafia' Don*, 113.

West. Many had gotten wealthy by buying, stealing, looting, extorting, or otherwise acquiring property formerly owned by the Soviet state. Some 9,000 criminal gangs with 35,000 members now controlled the majority of economic activity in the former Soviet Union. Fifteen Russian organized-crime groups were operating inside the U.S. Some invested in Manhattan real estate.

Vadim Trincher ran his extensive gambling ring out of Trump Tower raided by the FBI in April 2013. (NY Daily News)

In 1994, *Oleg Boiko*, a crony of Soviet leader Boris Yeltsin, purchased a suite in Trump Tower. Fifteen years later (2009), Vadim Trincher and his wife Elena obtained Boiko's Trump Tower apartment for $5 million cash. Several years later, the FBI arrested Trincher in an April 2013 raid on illegal gambling in Trump Tower.

In 2014, American courts sentenced Vadim Trincher to five years in prison (in Allentown, Pennsylvania) for racketeering and running illegal gambling operations out of Trump Tower and elsewhere since 2006. Trincher also laundered some $100 million in profits through Cyprus shell companies by issuing phony loan agreements. For 25 years, he used his Trump Tower residence as a safe house, an investment, and a gambling center.

Vyacheslav Ivankov, Thief-in-Law

In March 1992, Russian mafia boss *Vyacheslav "Yaponchik" Ivankov* (1940-2009) arrived in the U.S. to set up a money laundering network, rented a luxury condo in Trump Tower, and later moved to Trump Taj Mahal casino in Atlantic City, New Jersey, to avoid prosecution in New York. Ivankov was also a friend of *Alimzhan Tokhtakhounov*, a Putin crony involved in organized crime. Born in Tbilisi, Georgia, Ivankov was confined in 1974 in the Butyrki Prison in Moscow when he was "crowned" thief-in-law (*vor v zakone*) by other mafia members. *Vors* constitute an elite among Russian thieves and are greatly respected by the mafia and feared by the police. Ivankov was arrested for forgery, possession of firearms and drug trafficking in 1982. He was sentenced to 14 years in prison but was released in 1991 after serving a decade. Ivankov set up his new gang of about 100 members in Brighton Beach, the main mafia group in Brooklyn, with *Mikhail Sater* as a key leader.

To be a *vor v zakone* was a high honor among thieves. Vors were "crowned" with ritual tattoos in a prison culture that refused all cooperation with the authorities (guards), including work, helped other thieves, and later abandoned marriages, wives and children. In Trump Tower, Ivankov was a boss among thieves.

Brighton Beach was becoming the center of the Russian emigration in New York by the 90s. In June, 1992, the Silber brothers, Jewish mobsters from Odessa, opened a Russian restaurant in Brooklyn known as *Rasputin*, which became a mobster gathering place for both Russians and Italians. Gasoline bootlegging, extortion, and contract killings proliferated. On November 22, 1992, federal agents launched *Operation Red Daisy* against Russian mafia gangs in New York, New Jersey, Pennsylvania, and Florida. Many arrests were made, but the police remained cautious and fearful of the brutality of Russian mobsters whom they had to confront.

Wayne Barrett in his 1993 Trump biography *The Greatest Show on Earth*, concluded Trump's life intertwined with the underworld but paid little attention to Trump's extensive Russian and Eurasian mafia connections in telling his story.

In May 1994, the New York FBI office opened its C-24 squad to fight Russian organized crime. Ivankov presided over a "sit-down" meeting of Russian gangsters in Tel Aviv, Israel. He renewed ties with the gangs of Semion Mogilevich in Budapest and the Solntsevo Brotherhood mafia family of some 1,700 members in Moscow. Russia's Ministry of Interior informed the FBI that Ivankov was now in the U.S. and living in Trump Tower, a fact of which the FBI seems to have been ignorant.

Vyacheslav Ivankov (RT.com)

The Russian mafia flourished. In July 1994, Ivankov completed a drug deal with *Sergei Timofeyev*, who controlled Russian mafia operations in Cyprus. Ivankov by now managed a global network of crime that dealt in Russian oil, aluminum, weapons, and money laundering of tens of millions of dollars through U.S. and foreign banks.

But American authorities were watching. On June 8, 1995, the FBI arrested *Vyacheslav Ivankov* and charged him with extorting $3.5 million from a Russian investment company, Summit. Until 1995, the FBI had no idea for three years where Ivankov was living—in a luxury condo in Trump Tower. The FBI obtained a copy of Ivankov's personal telephone directory that included a working number for Trump

Organization's Trump Tower Residence and for a Trump Organization office FAX machine.

Punishment followed. In July 1996, Ivankov was found guilty of extortion and conspiracy. In early 1997, a federal court in New York sentenced Ivankov to 115 months in jail and five years on probation. A decade later, on July 13, 2009, *Vyacheslav Ivankov* was deported to Russia on murder and extortion charges stemming from the case of two Turks shot and killed in 1992 in Moscow. Ivankov died on October 9, 2009, in Moscow as a consequence of wounds suffered when shot by two Georgian mafia hit-men (snipers) on July 28, two weeks after his deportation from the U.S. and arrival in Russia.

Semion Mogilevich, FBI Most Wanted Crime Boss

By 1990, Ukrainian-born *Semion Mogilevich* headed a worldwide Eurasian and Russian organized crime network based in Prague and Budapest. (See above.) He was a 5' 6", 300-pound, ruthless criminal and avid chain smoker who headed a money laundering network that spanned more than 20 nations. He also had the charming habit of naming shell companies after his first wife, *Galina Telesh*. Although Mogilevich did not reside in Trump Tower, he was the boss of many organized crime members who did.

In 1993, when Trump divorced his wife Ivana and married his mistress, *Marla Maples*, the FBI finally established a Russian organized crime subsection in Washington D.C. to monitor mob activities and personnel. Over 300,000 Russian émigrés now lived in the greater New York area, especially Brighton Beach and Brooklyn. Eurasian organized crime families came to America from Moscow, Odessa, Tashkent, and Ekaterinburg. Many of them rented or purchased Trump properties as investments and safe havens, often unoccupied.

Semion Mogilevich began invading U.S. financial markets using a shell company called YBM Magnex International in Newtown, Pennsylvania, that supposedly manufactured magnets. Mogilevich was the majority shareholder. Company operations officer *Igor L'vovich*

Fisherman, 41, coordinated Mogilevich's organized crime empire from Budapest. Fisherman was a mathematician who once consulted for Chase Manhattan Bank. Dozens of other shell companies worked a giant money laundering operation. *Jacob Bogatin*, David's brother, prepared a public stock offering for YBM and in 1995 went to Canada to create a legal shell company for YBM called Pratecs Technologies, a blind pool, or business with no assets. Mogilevich met *Salvatore De-Falco*, the Italian mafia Camorra representative in the Czech Republic, for a conference in September 1993.

Kazakhs also got rich in Eurasian crime circles. In 1994, *Alexander Mashkevich* founded his European Resources Group of companies in mining, minerals, metals, gas, and smelting. Mashkevich, 40, was born in Kazakhstan and raised in Kirghizstan. He and *Patokh Chodiev* and *Alijan Ibragimov*, all Kazkhs, got control of chromium, aluminum, and natural gas operations in Kazakhstan under post-Soviet dictator *Nurultan Nazarbayev* and became billionaires in the Kazakh kleptocracy.

British intelligence periodically issued reports on the Mogilevich network of thousands of criminals from the U.K. to New Zealand, trafficking in stolen weapons, drugs, prostitutes, and art. Mogilevich's Philadelphia-based YBM Magnex scam to defraud investors of $150 million collapsed in May 1998. In August, the FBI produced a substantial internal report on Mogilevich and Eurasian organized crime that linked Mogilevich and Ivankov in a single worldwide enterprise. The FBI also concluded that Eurasian organized crime had contacts with the Genovese Cosa Nostra family in New York City.[20] Mogilevich planned to sell New York toxic waste cheaply in the area around Chernobyl. He fled Hungary in April 2000, days before the FBI established its Budapest Project there to investigate Eurasian organized crime.

---

[20] FBI, Department of Justice, "Semion Mogilevich Organization, Eurasian Organized Crime," Washington DC, August 1998. Garret M. Graff, *The Threat Matrix*, 561.

Semion Mogilevich

On April 24, 2003, the eastern district court of Pennsylvania in Philadelphia indicted Igor Fisherman on forty-five counts of *racketeering, securities and wire fraud, and money laundering* for the YBM scam and Mogilevich's network.

The FBI placed Mogilevich on its "most wanted fugitives" list on October 21, 2009, as a "Ukrainian businessman" charged with *racketeering, wire fraud, mail fraud, money laundering,* and other economic crimes worldwide.[21] He was also wanted for "alleged participation in a multi-million-dollar scheme to defraud investors in the stock of YBM Magnex International." Charges for *tax evasion* against Semion Mogilevich were dropped in Moscow in 2011. He vanished.

Fisherman later became a naturalized U.S. citizen and by 2012 was believed to be living in Moscow. In 2015, the FBI removed Mogilevich from its "most wanted" list after being so honored for six years. He now lives in Moscow or Hungary under FSB protection and

---

[21] B. Ross and M. Mosk, "Russian Mafia Boss Still at Large after FBI Wiretapping at Trump Tower," ABC News, March 21, 2007.

is unavailable to the FBI. According to Alexander Litvinenko, Mogilevich has been under Putin's protective wing (*krysha*) since the 1990s.[22]

Felix Sater, Stock Swindler and FBI Informant

In 1993, *Felix Sater*, 26, a Russian mobster, served a year in prison for stabbing a fellow stockbroker with a Margarita glass stem in a bar-room brawl at El Grande restaurant in Manhattan, requiring 110 stiches. Sater was also indicted for stock swindling and money laundering tied to the Gambino and Genovese crime families. The Sater (Sheferovsky) family had left Russia for Brooklyn (Brighton Beach) in 1974 when Felix was eight. His father, *Mikhail Sater*, headed the Russian mafia in Brooklyn, having served prison time in England for counterfeiting and fraud before coming to the U.S. Felix joined Ivankov's White Rock Partners' mobbed-up investment group after attending courses at Pace University, dropping out, and making his living selling stocks for Bear Stearns and other companies until barred in 1993 because of his assault conviction. In 1994, Sater opened his own firm at 40 Wall St. (a building owned by Trump) and began laundering money for the mob. He and Salvatore Laurie got control of White Rock Partners, renamed it State Street Capital and fleeced elderly Jews of some $40 million with various pump-and-dump stock schemes.[23]

Mikhail Sater worked for Semion Mogilevich, the Ukrainian-born boss of Russian bosses whose assets include nuclear material and weapons from the Soviet military. Approached by the terrorist group al Qaida for arms, Mogilevich had been a friend of Vladimir Putin since Leningrad days. By 1992, he was wanted for *arms dealing, murder, extortion, drug dealing, prostitution, mail and wire fraud, and false SEC filings* in the U.S. Mogilevich now became the main financier of what the FBI called Russian-based organized crime (RBOC).

---

[22] Luke Harding, *A Very Expensive Poison. The Definitive Story of the Murder of Litvinenko and Russia's War with the West* (London: Guardian Books, 2016) 355.

[23] On Felix Sater's links to Trump, see Johnston, *Trump* 162-6. Also, see Salvatore Lauria, *The Scorpion and the Frog* (Beverly Hills: New Millennium Press, 2003, 67-8, 166, 173, 209, 238, where Felix Sater is disguised as Lex Tersa, and Glushakow, '*Mafia Don*,' 82-88.

T R U M P

FELIX H. SATER
SENIOR ADVISOR TO
DONALD TRUMP

THE TRUMP ORGANIZATION
725 FIFTH AVENUE • NEW YORK, N.Y. 10022
PHONE: +1 212-715-███ • FAX: +1 ███ ███ ████
MOBILE: +1 ███ ███ ████ • EMAIL: FSATER@TRUMPORG.COM

Felix Sater's business card for the Trump Organization. (Forbes)

In 1998, the FBI recruited Mikhail Slater's son Felix as an informant and "cooperating witness." His handlers included *Leo Taddeo*, head of Russian and Italian sections of the Manhattan FBI office, and *Gary Uher*. Uher later (June 2015) began working for security on the Donald Trump presidential campaign. Felix Sater reported daily for 10 years to the FBI from his Trump Tower office, where he worked for Trump developing new hotels around the country.

In November 1996, Donald Trump visited Moscow with his friend *Howard Lorber*, announcing plans to invest $250 million in Russian hotels, but did nothing more than apply for Russian trademarks. Trump met *Igor Ballo*, president of the Moscow Gaming Business Association (1992) and owner of the *Beverly Hills* (*Firebird*) casino in Moscow. But Trump's plans came to nothing. Trump was angry because he could not buy private land for hotels in Russia. He met Moscow mayor *Yury Luzhkov* and discussed commercial plans for Moscow. But all the deals fell through. In Russia, Trump the businessman was a loser.

But in New York, Trump was a winner. In August 1998, Russia defaulted on $40 billion of domestic debt. The Russian stock market collapsed. Russian oligarchs and criminals scrambled to find safe haven in the New York real estate market. Trump did business with many of them and sold some of them retail space or residences in Trump Tower, by now a well-known safe haven for Eurasian organized crime. He needed no Russian investments himself to profit from those Russians who did invest in Trump properties.

By October, Trump World Tower apartment units (scheduled to open in 2001) were selling to new buyers, about one-third of them Russian individuals or companies. They included Georgian *Tamir Sapir* and Ukrainian *Sam Kislin*, who partnered to sell Trump 200 TVs (on credit) for his new building. Kislin soon became a fund-raiser for mayor *Rudy Giuliani*, known for successfully prosecuting the Cosa Nostra in NYC.

On December 10, 1998, Felix Sater pleaded guilty to one count of *racketeering and fraud* in the $40 million stock fraud case.[24] Sater avoided jail by becoming an FBI informant on the Russian mafia. Sater signed a "cooperation agreement" with the Eastern District of NY (EDNY) federal attorney *Andrew Weissmann* (later on Robert Mueller's investigating team) under attorney *Loretta Lynch*. Reportedly Sater helped purchase Stinger missiles for the CIA on the Russian arms market to keep them out of the hands of Al Quaeda. Sater was thus a "cooperating witness" who received a "federal defense of immunity" for his services. Attorney for EDNY Loretta Lynch was informed and involved, but unforthcoming about her star witness, who wore a court-ordered ankle bracelet much of the time. Sater stayed safe as a cooperating witness for the FBI until 2009, protected as a matter of "national security."

Trump finally settled the long-running (since 1983) case of the Trump Tower Polish workers and the Homewreckers Union pension fund in 1999. The settlement was sealed by court, and its terms are unknown. A year later, Roger Stone chaired a Trump exploratory advisory team on a prospective run for U.S. president that never materialized. Trump seemed oddly immune to prosecution.

In 2001, Robert Hanssen, Soviet spy and FBI mole, was arrested for treason and espionage. He is now serving fifteen consecutive life sentences in federal prison in Colorado. Whether or not the FBI has interviewed Hanssen about his work on wiretapping Trump Tower

---

[24] U.S. v. Felix Sater, Criminal Docket No. 98 CR 1101 (ILG).

remains to be seen. The new FBI director at the end of 2001 was Robert F. Mueller, the current special counsel with full knowledge of the Hanssen espionage case and the FBI's work in Manhattan.

Helly Nahmad, Preet Bharara, and the Trump Tower Raid

Lebanese-American art dealer *Helly Nahmad*, 21, began buying up Floor 51 of Trump Tower in 1999. The project took a decade and cost $20 million. Nahmad, owner of his father's Helly Nahmad Gallery, was arrested in April 2013 for running a massive illegal gambling operation in Trump Tower and laundering money via Cyprus. Trump's father and real estate mentor Fred Trump died later that year.

Another illegal gambler in Trump Tower was *Anatoly Golubchik*, the head of an offshore company called Lytton Ventures, Inc., linked to Semion Mogilevich.

In 2011, French art dealer Phillipe Maestracci sued the Helly Nahmad Gallery over the ownership of Modigliani's *Seated Man with a Cane*, a painting considered by some to be Holocaust looted art. Nahmad argued he did not own the painting, which belonged to International Art Center S.A. (IAC) of Panama, a shell company formed in 1995 by his uncle, Giuseppe Nahmad. But by 2011, the sole owner of IAC was Helly's father, David Nahmad.

Meanwhile, the FBI obtained a warrant to wiretap Trump Tower in order to monitor an extensive Russian *money laundering* and *gambling* network operating from unit 63A. That network moved some $50 million into the U.S. illegally. Among the 30 people indicted were Helly Nahmad and Russian mafia boss, *Alimzhan Tokhtakhounov*, who escaped the U.S. and became a fugitive from U.S. justice in Moscow. German regulators gave ownership of the Bank of Cyprus to Russian oligarchs (like Dmitry Rybolovlev), who owned a majority of shares and turned the bank into an important offshore node in the Eurasian money laundering network.

*Vadim Trincher and gambling friends escorted from Trump Tower
by FBI agents, April 16, 2013.* (NY Times)

On April 16, 2013, *Preet Bharara*, U.S. attorney's office, Southern District of New York (SDNY), issued warrants to arrest the thirty Trump Tower Russians for *money laundering* and illegal sports *gambling* out of Trump Tower. The FBI arrested them individually in various U.S. cities. The group included Helly Nahmad, Vadim Trincher, and Alimzhan Tokhtakhounov. Nahmad had also laundered money through Cyprus shell companies and banks via wire transfers to U.S. real estate and hedge funds.

Preet Bharara graduated from Harvard College and Columbia Law School and became the U.S. attorney for the Southern District in 2009 (Trump fired him on March 11, 2017). Nominated by President Obama and confirmed by the U.S. Senate on May 15, 2009, Bharara quickly became the crusader prosecutor of corruption and Wall St. white-collar crime, and thus a definite threat to Trump. In June 2017, Bharara said there was sufficient evidence to begin an *obstruction of justice* case against the novice U.S. president for his firing of FBI director James Comey.

Bharara had broken up another $230 million Russian money-laundering operation in NYC. The tax refund fraud began in 2008 with Russian investments in real estate—four luxury condos and commercial buildings in Manhattan. In this case, the buildings were purchased by *Prevezon*, a real estate holding company in Cyprus with money laundered through shell companies in Moldova, owned by *Denis Katsyv*. Katsyv's attorney, *Natalia Veselnitskaya*, would turn up again during the Trump campaign for a secret meeting in Trump Tower arranged by Donald Trump Jr. and his friend Emin Agalarov, an Azeri-Russian rock singer.

Sergei Magnitsky, a Russian tax attorney and whistle-blower in the tax refund case, was found dead in his Moscow jail cell in November 2009. The U.S. Magnitsky Rule of Law Accountability Act (2012), passed by Congress, barred 60 Russians tied to Magnitsky's death from ever entering the U.S. The Russian government consequently in December 2012 forbade the U.S. adoption of Russian children and, in April 2013, prevented 18 Americans, including Bharara, from entering Russia. But the real focus of the case was money laundering.

Bharara also closed down the *Rasputin* restaurant at 2670 Coney Island Ave. in Brooklyn, a long-time hangout for Russian mobsters, on May 22, 2013. The restaurant owner *Michael Levitis* was arrested for fraud involving his Mission Settlement Agency. Bharara considered Levitis a criminal, indicted in 2011 for lying to the FBI. He indicted Levitis now for defrauding more than a thousand customers in his bogus debt relief operation of some $2.2 million. On November 20, 2014, a SDNY judge sentenced Levitis to nine years in prison and a $4 million fine. He pleaded guilty to *conspiracy* and *wire fraud.*

In April 2013, another Trump Tower resident mobster, *Vadim Trincher*, was sentenced to five years in prison; his release date was July 2017. Helly Nahmad served five months in prison, as did Anatoly Golubchik.

Alimzhan Tokhtakhounov, Fraud and Money Laundering

In 2001, Russian mafia boss *Alimzhan Tokhtakhounov* bribed judges to fix an ice skating competition at the impending Squaw Valley winter Olympics. An Uzbek crime boss from Tashkent, he ultimately lived in Trump Tower, unit 63A, duly wiretapped by the FBI. He made his millions laundering money through his Moscow casinos—Metropol, Evropa, and Aziia. And he joined many other Russian mafia tenants running illegal gambling operations out of Trump Tower.[25]

Alimzhan Tokhtakhounov in his friendly Tiger T-shirt.
(worldstopmost.com)

In October 2009, Felix Sater was finally sentenced to up to 20 years in jail for *stock manipulation* and *fraud* in late 1990s. In fact, Sater paid a $25,000 fine and served no jail time because of his contributions to the FBI and CIA as a cooperating witness and informant. Mafia boss *Semion Mogilevich*, 53, escaped to Russia and was arrested in 2008 in Moscow for tax evasion, released from prison July 2009, and then appeared on the FBI's most wanted list of criminals for *wire fraud, murder, money laundering, false SEC filings* and other crimes. When his partner, Ernest Mendes, threatened to expose his criminal past, Felix Sater telephoned Mendes and said he would electrocute his testicles, cut off his legs, and leave what remained of Mendes' body in a car trunk.[26] Mendes was understandably silent after that.

---

[25] On the Trump Tower Russians, see Craig Unger, "Trump's Russian Laundromat," *The New Republic,* July 13, 2017.

[26] Glushakow, *'Mafia' Don,* 84-5.

In 2013, *Alimzhan Tokhtakhounov* disappeared in Moscow. He had run a profitable gambling and money laundering operation out of Trump Tower. FBI agent *Mike Gaeta*, who headed the FBI Eurasian organized crime office in New York, called him a "major player" in Russian organized crime. "It was as if all criminal roads led to Trump Tower," retired MI-6 officer Christopher Steele confided to friends.[27] And Steele—a friend of Gaeta—seemed to have it right. He and Gaeta would both play a major role five years later in tracking down Trump's ties with Russian oligarchs and criminals.

Mikhail Khodorkovsky, Fraud and Tax Evasion

Vladimir Putin with Mikhail Khodorkovsky, Russia's richest oligarch in 2002, before Khodorkovsky's arrest and trial.

In 2003, Transparency International ranked Russia more corrupt than 64 percent of the world's nations. In 2010, it ranked Russia more corrupt than 86 percent of the world. More than a decade after the collapse of the Soviet Union, the USSR had dissolved into a series of authoritarian nations dominated by corrupt leaders, kleptocratic

---

[27] Jane Mayer, "The Man Behind the Dossier," *The New Yorker*, March 12, 2018, 54.

elites, and organized crime families. The line between the Russian government and organized crime was fluid, flexible and changing—when it existed at all.

Vladimir Putin, despite a vicious war in Chechnya, was re-elected Russian president in 2004 with 71 percent of the vote, compared with 53 percent in 2000. His handpicked successor *Dmitry Medvedev* received over 70 percent of the vote in 2008 and promptly named Putin his prime minister in a pre-arranged non-transfer of power.

Putin was determined to show that the oligarchs and criminals were not beyond the reach of his government. In 2003, the wealthiest oligarch in Russia, *Mikhail Khodorkovsky*, 42, was sentenced to nine years in a prison camp for *fraud and tax evasion*. The Russian-Jewish Khodorkovsky, a chemical engineer and a communist party member, had his own bank, Menatep, before he was 25. He later acquired the oil company Yukos. His attorney was *Robert Amsterdam*, 40, a Canadian international human rights lawyer, who soon found, as a foreigner, that he was disbarred from practicing in Russia.

In June 2005, Putin pocketed the diamond Super Bowl ring of New England Patriots owner, Robert Kraft, in St. Petersburg. In September, Putin stole a glass replica of an AK-47 Kalashnikov rifle from the Guggenheim Museum in New York. Putin regularly exhibited *pleonexia*, the insatiable desire to have what belongs to someone else. He is a thief that can't help himself. And he had the power to put the richest man in Russia in jail.

In 2007, Russian analyst Stanislas Belkovsky estimated Putin's personal net worth at $40 billion. Today estimates run up to $200 billion. Most of this capital is lodged in overseas shell companies headed nominally by Putin's childhood friend from Leningrad, the cellist *Sergei Roldugin*, or by other Putin cronies in banks, stock or real estate.

Putin's front man, cellist Sergei Rodulgin

In March 2009, Khodorkovsky went on trial in Moscow for the second time for *embezzlement* and *money laundering*. Robert Amsterdam, as a foreign attorney, was not allowed to plead his client's case in Russia.

Aleksei Navalny, Putin's popular rival, in 2010 dubbed Russia's kleptocracy "The Party of Crooks and Thieves." Navalny was later convicted on a trumped-up fraud charge and banned from running against Putin for president in March 2018. (Putin had Navalny arrested shortly before the elections, just in case, but then released him.) Khodorkovsky was found guilty again on the new charges and returned to prison. Then, in 2013, Putin unexpectedly pardoned Khodorkovsky, who promptly moved to Switzerland. Khodorkovsky relaunched his Open Russia organization for reform in 2014 and visited the U.S. As far as we know, he did not live in Trump Tower.

By 2012, the largest (11 percent) tenant in Trump Tower was the Industrial and Commercial Bank of China (ICBC), whose U.S. headquarters took up the twentieth floor. The lease covered 20,404 square feet and cost $1.95 million per year. Trump boasted about the fact in 2015, but there was still some question as to whether or not the ICBC lease violated the emoluments clause of the U.S. Constitution after

Trump became president. At any rate, Trump had no problem hosting paying Chinese bankers in his hotel.

On February 28, 2016, presidential candidate Ted Cruz claimed that Trump was "terrified to release his taxes" because "there have been multiple media reports about Donald's business dealings with the mob, with the mafia."[28] Cruz's comment was a rare example of political opponents willing to speak out on Donald Trump's decades-long ties to organized crime, American, Russian, and Eurasian. And the hub of those ties remained the casino, investment opportunity and Eurasian crime safe house known as Trump Tower.[29]

---

[28] Ted Cruz on "Meet the Press," February 28, 2016.

[29] According to *Forbes* magazine, in 2018 Donald J. Trump owned 244,000 square feet of Trump Tower, valued at $471 million with a debt load of $100 million. The value of Trump's TT holdings declined in 2015-8 by $159 million. Trump also owns a debt-free penthouse in the building worth $90 million.

THE MONEY TRAIL

3. DONALD J. TRUMP, BANKRUPT

1990 was probably the worst year in my history.
—Donald J. Trump

Trump was never as wealthy as he claimed. His net worth estimates run from $150 million to $11 billion. He borrowed money at will but often did not repay his loans or pay his bills. He was well known for stiffing his customers and lenders. Yet in 1985, banks continued to loan money to Trump for building projects, believing that the Hyatt, Trump Tower, and Trump Plaza of Atlantic City were all solid investments. Trump purchased the Hilton Hotel ($320 million) and Harrah's share of his Trump Plaza casino ($250 million) with various bank loans.

Trump later boasted that his father Fred left him "a relatively small amount of money (compared to where I am today—over $10 billion) but a vast amount of knowledge."[30] In fact, Trump squandered whatever money he inherited from his father, borrowed money from banks whenever he could, and had to ask his father to bail him out of debt on several occasions. And what Trump did not know, he either made up or lied about.

In 1984, Trump purchased his first casino, Harrah's at Trump

---

[30] TTA, December 7, 2013.

Plaza, in Atlantic City, New Jersey, where casino gambling had been legal since 1977. He began to do business with gangsters active in the gaming industry there and in Las Vegas. He built a casino gambling empire on credit, but failed to make nearly as much money as his competitors did. When the casino industry in general was thriving, Trump's casinos curiously failed and lost money.

Only borrowed money enabled Trump to purchase Mar- a-Lago, the Florida estate of heiress Marjorie Merriweather Post. We saw that Post bequeathed the 58-bedroom mansion to the U.S. Department of the Interior as a presidential retreat just before her death in 1973. The white elephant ate up federal money and languished. Returned to the Post Family Foundation by the Interior Department in 1981, the estate was deteriorating at taxpayer expense when Trump decided to purchase the aging mansion at a bargain price of less than $10 million. [31]

On December 27, 1985, Trump purchased Mar-a-Lago with a home mortgage loan from Chase Manhattan Bank that oddly went unrecorded at the local courthouse.[32] The price for Mar-a-Lago was $9 million. Trump took out a mortgage loan of $8 million from Chase Manhattan Bank and deposited $400,000 from other bank loans. Trump put up only $2,800 of his own money as a deposit. Trump also purchased floors 66-68 of Trump Tower that year, probably with another bank loan. Bank loans and mortgages seemed to underwrite all of Trump's luxury purchases.

In 1986, the *NYTimes* reported that 251 of 268 apartments in Trump Tower had now been sold for $277 million. Trump's media campaign spread fake news that the British royal family members would buy into Trump Tower. They did not. On a personal note, Trump's family attorney and political mentor Roy Cohn died of AIDS in July, a short time after being disbarred in New York. Trump held a farewell party for Cohn and a few friends at Mar-a-Lago on March 1, at which the dying mob attorney was well feted by his disciple.

---

[31] On Trump's purchase of Mar a Lago with bank loans, see Barrett, *Trump* 313-23. Mar a Lago in 2018 is worth $150 million and has no debt. Its value declined since 2015 by $50 million, according to *Forbes* magazine.

[32] Johnston, *Trump*, 5, 81-2.

A year later, Tony Schwartz ghost-authored Trump's nominal book *The Art of the Deal* (1987), which Trump later praised, slammed, or claimed he wrote, depending on the situation.

Meanwhile Cohn's client, the Gambino mafia family, was in turmoil. John Gotti (1940-2002) murdered Paul Castellano in a drug war in late 1985 and took over the family's operations. Gotti dominated the New York crime scene until 1992, when he was convicted of five murders, racketeering, obstruction of justice, illegal gambling, extortion, tax evasion, and loan sharking. Gotti received a life sentence.

Trump had his own problems with the mob. In 1988, Trump tried to seduce Edith Creamer, the daughter of one of Gotti's mob friends, *Robert LiButti* (1932-2014), a race-horse broker and high roller at Trump casinos in Las Vegas and Atlantic City. LiButti was known as an obnoxious and abusive racist and misogynist gangster who insisted Trump fire all his African-American and female blackjack dealers. When he heard that Trump was coming on to his daughter, Libutti reportedly said: "Donald, I'll f—ing pull your balls from your legs," a credible threat.

Trump and LiButti nonetheless maintained their longtime relationship for years. When Trump claimed he could barely remember who LiButti was, Edith responded "He's a liar."[33]

Trump purchased the Taj Mahal in Atlantic City in 1988. Lacking money to complete construction, Trump obtained a billion dollars by selling junk bonds repayable with an interest rate of 14 percent, or $140 million annually that Trump could not afford. The New Jersey Gaming Commission in 1991 investigated a Trump casino and fined it $450,000 for giving three luxury cars to LiButti, a known mobster. But LiButti plunked down over $11 million in losings at Trump Plaza casino from 1986 to 1989, to Trump's advantage. The New Jersey Casino Control Commission then fined Trump $200,000 for violating anti-discrimination laws.[34]

Trump also purchased the *Trump Princess*, a massive yacht built in 1980 for $100 million and owned by Saudi billionaire arms merchant Adnan Kashoggi and the Sultan of Brunei. By the time Trump

[33] Johnston, *Trump*, 195-202.

[34] Glubashow, 92, 161.

acquired the vessel in 1989, the price was down to $29 million for a used boat. Trump sold it in 1991 for $20 million and thus lost another $9 million on yet another failed deal that was forced on him by a bankruptcy settlement.

By 1990, Donald Trump was virtually bankrupt. He owed more than $4 billion to 70 banks. He later confessed "1990 was probably the worst year in my history." Trump was sued 21 times that year. In 1991, his Taj Mahal casino in Atlantic City filed for Chapter 11 *bankruptcy*. In 1992, his other Atlantic City casinos and his Plaza Hotel in New York also filed for bankruptcy. Five projects in Russia failed to materialize, and U.S. banks refused to loan him any more money. At about this time, various Russians began financing his projects, buying or renting his real estate, and keeping him out of bankruptcy. Trump enterprises owed $9 billion in debts, forcing Trump to carry $300 million in annual loan payments, which he often failed to make.

Trump was now really bankrupt, but few knew it. In August 1990, New Jersey casino regulators estimated Trump's overall debt at $3.4 billion, adding that a complete financial collapse of the Trump organization was possible. Trump's personal debt was $975 million. His net worth as determined by an accounting firm hired by the banks was negative—he owed his lenders an aggregate $295 million more than his total investment income. Russian investment capital would be most welcome for Trump to survive financially. His net worth was less than zero.[35]

Faced with financial ruin, Trump tried to borrow $100 million from a banking consortium led by Citibank. But his alleged fortune was a house of cards built entirely on credit and loans. He owed $85 million in monthly interest payments on a billion-dollar debt. To get more loans, Trump had to pledge as security all that he owned. A new Trump financial officer was hired who reported directly to the banks, not to Trump. Yet Trump's bank-restricted income was not shabby: $450,000 per month! The liquidity crisis was temporarily resolved, but Trump's financial vulnerability had been exposed.

[35] Johnston, *Trump*, 88-90.

He was a bankrupt financial and business failure, whatever his protestations to the contrary.

Finally, in June 1990, Trump signed off on an agreement with the banks in the only way he could pay off a $1.3 billion debt in his Taj Mahal casino junk bonds, that was only part of his total debt. His father, Fred Trump, also bailed him out when he missed interest payments on his $3.5 billion debt for Trump Castle. The Taj Mahal then filed for bankruptcy.

At this point, both the Soviet Union and Trump's marriage to Ivana were in the process of collapse. Massive amounts of former Soviet government property vanished into private hands in the new Russia and sought safe investment abroad, often in Trump properties. Putin and his family moved back to Leningrad and began to look for opportunities other than the KGB. He ended up working in the mayor's office of *Anatoly Sobchak* on the sale and disposal of Soviet properties abroad. In this capacity, Putin had dealings with Russian mobsters, including Mogilevich and members of the Tambov and Taganskaia mafia families.

Many wealthy Russians sought jobs, residences, and gambling options in Trump properties. There were so many Russians at the Taj Mahal in 1994, that Trump hired a Russian rock star couple, *Philip Kirkorov* and *Alla Pugacheva* (then husband and wife) to give a gala concert at the Taj. Kirkorov soon became a great fan of Trump, both as casino owner and future presidential candidate. Trump called Kirkorov Russia's Michael Jackson. There were hugs all around when the two men met at the Moscow Miss Universe Contest in 2013, where Kirkorov was a pageant judge. Kirkorov, an alleged assaulter of women who was Bulgarian-born, maintained his rock star status in Russia, where Putin presented him with the Order of Honor on November 17, 2017.

But there was more bad news for Trump. In April 1990, Judge Charles Stewart Jr. of SDNY found Trump and his companies guilty of "a conspiracy to deprive the [Housewreckers Union pension] funds of their rightful contribution" by underpaying illegal Polish workers on the Trump Tower demolition job. The Polish Brigade seemed to be winning, although its case was settled only in 1999 for an unknown fee, probably around $4 million. No wonder Trump abandoned his old telephone pseudonym "John Barron" in favor of a new one, "John Miller." Barron had been quoted in the court case, but Miller had not. Once again, there was a real John Miller, 32, an ABC investigative reporter who interviewed Osama bin Laden in 1998 and later served as assistant director of public affairs for the FBI and then deputy commissioner for the NYPD. Miller's father was also a close friend of *Frank Costello* (1891-1973), the most powerful mobster in New York.

Trump's phony "John Miller" conducted an extensive telephone interview in 1991 with Sue Carswell of *People Magazine* about Trump's lascivious personal life, posing as Trump's PR man. Trump lied without shame using his fake news alias. Carswell destroyed her tapes of the conversations, but Trump's tapes later found their way to the *Washington Post*. His use of pseudonyms continued to mimic tools used by both the FBI and the mob: deception, disinformation, and entrapment.

Donald and Ivana Trump divorced in 1992, the year Bill Clinton was elected U.S. president. Ivana promptly published a novel entitled *For Love Alone*. Trump immediately sued for $25 million in damages to his brand on the grounds that the novel was based on their marriage and violated the nondisclosure section of their divorce degree. The couple settled the case for an undisclosed sum in 1993. Trump's personal debt stood at $900 million, and the Taj Mahal lost another $550 million and went into bankruptcy a second time. Trump's book, *Surviving at the Top*, produced a 1992 *MAD* magazine cartoon about the banks who had "restructured" his debt and helped conceal the fact that Trump was quite simply broke. His 1995 tax return (courtesy of his wife, Marla Maples) showed he lost $916 million that year.

Trump never admitted this, of course. In 2015, he tweeted: "Stop saying I went bankrupt. I never went bankrupt but like many great business people have used the laws to corporate advantage—smart!"[36]

[36] TTA, June 19, 2015.

Fraud and Money Laundering

In 1995, the U.S. Treasury Department's Financial Crime Enforcement Network fined the Trump Taj Mahal in Atlantic City $477,700 for currency reporting transaction violations, i.e. *money laundering*. By 2004, Trump Hotels and Casinos Resorts carried a $1.8 billion debt and filed for Chapter 11 bankruptcy following the 2008 recession. Financial analysts learned that the Trump Hotels and Resorts lost 89 percent of their value between 1995 and 2005, whereas the Dow Jones Casino Index gained 160 percent. No one seemed to know why. Nor did they know who was covering Trump's enormous and unusual losses.

Trump hired attorney *Marc Kasowitz* in 2001 to restructure the debt on his Atlantic City casinos. Kasowitz, 49, was a Yale and Cornell graduate whose clients now included the sanctioned Russian Sberbank and Ukrainian billionaire *Oleg Deripaska*, a friend and client of Paul Manafort. Kasowitz defended the Port Authority on charges of negligence by victims of 9/11 in 2005 but lost the case. He then resurfaced in 2017 to defend Trump in the matter of Russian interference in the 2016 presidential election.

Nothing went Trump's way. By 2004, Trump Taj Mahal was $1.8 billion in debt; Trump filed for bankruptcy. Trump Mortgage was established in 2006. A year and a half later, when that company collapsed, Trump denied any involvement himself. Meanwhile, his company Trump Steaks died a quiet death as well. And Trump was compelled to use yet another alias, "David Dennison," in his dalliances with prostitutes and porn stars. But such deceptions fooled no one.

Trump Entertainment Resorts filed for bankruptcy (the sixth bankruptcy filing for Trump) after the 2008 recession. Trump defaulted on a $640 million construction loan for an unbuilt Trump hotel in Chicago. Another luxury hotel project in Dubai folded. The FBI office in Moscow reported in April that Russian organized crime figures, notably *Evgeny Doskin* and *Konstantin Ginzburg*, were moving into South Florida. In their investigations, the FBI focussed on *fraud* and *money laundering*.

The failures continued. Trump Hollywood, a $355 million oceanfront condominium in Florida, was foreclosed on in 2010. The Trump

Ocean Resort in Baja, Mexico, went broke before construction even began. Then there was the Taj Mahal.

The Trump Taj Mahal in Atlantic City, New Jersey, was fined $10 million in 2015 for failing to report suspicious financial transactions. The casino had long been a preferred gathering place for Russian mafia mobsters, according to the FBI, and had declared bankruptcy in 2014. The Taj was under investigation for *money laundering* again in 2017. The year before, in 2016, Trump dumped his problem and sold the bankrupt Taj Mahal casino in Atlantic City to his old crony, hedge-fund manager *Carl Icahn*, who closed the casino down after 26 years of operation. Icahn was later named special adviser to the president. Trump was rid of the Taj Mahal, if not Icahn, who served briefly as a White House adviser in 2017.

From 1996 to 2007, Trump filed unsuccessfully for hotel and branding deals in Russia with Rospatent, the Russian government's patent agency. He received decade-long trademarks, but no actual deals except the short-lived Trump Vodka. In 2016, he consolidated all his trademarks in the DTTM Operations holding company in Delaware. By April 2017, Trump had 157 trademark applications pending in 36 countries, including Russia. Between April and December 2016, all his Russian trademarks were renewed for 10 years (four of them on Election Day). They are all consolidated under DTTM.

In 2005, Trump borrowed $650 million from *Deutsche Bank*, his New York creditor that had a branch bank in Moscow since 1881. Coincidentally, the bank also had a New York branch office that sat on the land of Trump's grandfather, Friedrich Trumpf (1869-1918), who owned and ran a barbershop. In a 50-story, 1980s skyscraper at 60 Wall St., Deutsche Bank was the only bank left that would loan Trump money, even though the bank estimated Trump's net worth as a meagerly $640 million when he claimed it to be $3.6 billion. With the financial crisis of 2008, Trump defaulted on his payments. He still owed Deutsche Bank $330 million. Instead of paying off his bank loan, Trump countersued the bank for $3 billion in damages. A judge threw out Trump's suit. In 2010, Trump shifted his loan requests from Deutsche Bank's real estate division to its private wealth division. To his delight, his new division renewed his $330 million loan and added another $25-50 million for good measure. By the time Trump became U.S. president, he still owed Deutsche Bank some $300 million in four loans due in 2023 and 2024.

Meanwhile, Deutsche Bank was caught laundering money for the Russians. The bank worked through *Andrei Kostin*, a former Soviet diplomat and alleged KGB spy whom Putin made head of Vneshtorgbank (VTB), an international state bank that in 2005 acquired the Moscow Narodny Bank (based in London) and the Eurobank (based in Paris). Deutsche Bank hired Kostin's son in 2007 and made a series of profitable trades with VTB. Felix Sater noted that VTB had once agreed to finance a Moscow Trump Tower that never materialized.

Between 2011 and 2015, an American banker named *Tim Wiswell* worked for Alfa Bank in Moscow, run by Trump's friend *Mikhail Friedman*, then moved over to Deutsche Bank and ran a money laundering scheme out of the bank's Moscow office. He used mirror trades abroad to move money out of Russia. In August 2015, Deutsche Bank fired Wiswell, and he and his family disappeared to Southeast Asia. Regulators in London and New York penalized Deutsche Bank with fines of £163 million and $475 million. Latvian officials shut down another money laundering operation in Moldova in 2016.

In addition to The Donald, Deutsche Bank had accounts for daughter Ivanka Trump, her husband Jared Kushner, and Kushner's mother, Seryl Stadtmauer. Kushner opened a $25 million account with the bank and received another construction loan of $285 million in 2016 on the building Kushner purchased from *Lev Leviev*. Deutsche Bank also loaned Trump money for the old Post Office Building in Washington D.C., now a Trump hotel, the Doral golf course in Florida, and a Chicago office building. On December 5, 2017, special prosecutor Robert Mueller issued a subpoena of Deutsche Bank financial records related to the Trump family.

In October 2013, Trump faced a class action suit for *fraud* and *racketeering* because he promised but delivered "neither Donald Trump nor a university." After much loud protesting that the federal judge in San Diego U.S. District Court was born in Mexico, and therefore unfair to Trump, Trump was elected U.S. president. He promptly settled the case of the fraudulent Trump University for $25 million and thus escaped prison under a RICO racketeering charge.[37] We do not know how Trump came up with the money to settle.

After 1990, Trump escaped financial ruin only with Russian and Eurasian money. If American banks were dumping him as not creditworthy, he desperately needed new sources of income for his massive, confusing and overlapping network of companies. He found those new sources in Eurasian organized crime, whose capital flight from the former Soviet Union sought safe haven in the New York real estate market. And he became increasingly friendly with millionaire (and billionaire) oligarchs operating within the Russian kleptocracy. Vladimir Putin ran his own suspect foreign trade operations out of the mayor's office in Leningrad.

In 2017, *Forbes* magazine estimated Trump's net worth at $3.5 billion and gave him a rank of 544 among the world's richest individuals. That same year some $31.3 billion left Russia for foreign banks and individuals, up 160 percent from 2016. Trump was rich and getting richer on Russian and Eurasian money laundered through his real estate empire. Trump went from bankrupt to billionaire without anyone knowing precisely how much money he actually had, where it originated, or where it was hidden. As Eric Trump put it in 2013, "We don't rely on American banks. We have all the funding we need out of Russia."[38]

---

[37] Art Cohen v. Donald J. Trump, October 18, 2013, under RICO.

[38] Jeffrey Toobin, "The Miss Universe Contest," *The New Yorker*, March 12, 2018, 54.

Donald Trump, Tevfik Arif and Felix Sater,
September 19, 2007. (NY Times)

4. JARED KUSHNER, FELIX SATER, AND TRUMP SoHo

Felix Sater, boy, I have to even think about it.
—Donald Trump, 2013

Well, we had a tenant in Trump Tower called Bayrock,
and Bayrock was interested in getting us into deals.
—Donald Trump, 2013 deposition under oath

Trump SoHo was a much-touted luxury apartment building in Manhattan funded by Russian and Kazakh oligarchs and criminals that also served as a money laundry for Trump through a shell company called Bayrock and its Trump subsidiaries. The main engineer of the operation was Felix Sater.

Felix Sater, a Donald Trump employee, grew up in the Crown Heights area of Brooklyn and, in time, became a convert to *Chabad*, a Hasidic Jewish sect of Lubavitcher believers founded in 1775 in Lithuania. The Lubavitchers survived until the Nazi Holocaust swept across Eastern Europe and wiped out many of their villages in what became Belarus and Poland, as well as Lithuania. In 1951, the enterprising Rabbi Schneerson transformed Chabad into a movement with thousands of synagogues and other organizations worldwide. Persecuted in Imperial Russia and the Soviet Union, the Lubavitchers were welcomed after 1991 in the new Russia. Many of them emigrated to the U.S. and joined their co-religionists in Brooklyn, especially the Republican and conservative Crown Heights section. The Kushner family ended up in New Jersey.

In 1998, *Loretta Lynch*, 39 (Harvard Law School, 1984), became the U.S. Attorney for EDNY with federal prosecutor responsibilities for Brooklyn, Queens, Staten Island, and Long Island. That December, she worked with the FBI to arrange cooperation with Felix Sater on national security issues and the conviction of 20 Cosa Nostra figures. Sater thus became a cooperating FBI witness with immunity from federal prosecution. Officially, Sater was identified simply as "John Doe."

Tevfik Arif, FBI Informant

Not all of the Eurasian mobsters were Russians. Many were Kazakhs. In 1989, a Kazakh named *Tevfik Arif* founded his Bayrock Group LLC in Moscow. Arif was a Kazakh real estate developer, former deputy director of USSR Ministry of Commerce and Trade's department of hotel management. Sensing imminent Soviet collapse, Arif moved Bayrock from Moscow to Kazakhstan in 1990. In 1993, Arif resigned his posts and shifted his companies to Turkey, where he owned a jewelry business. In time, Arif moved operations from Tashkent to Moscow to Istanbul, then to New York, where he met Felix Sater and Donald Trump.[39]

Arif was not Jewish, but he owned a mansion in Port Washington, where he became a generous supporter of Felix Sater and the local Chabad House.

Arif moved his Bayrock businesses from Kazakhstan to the U.S. in 2000 and hired Felix Sater to run Bayrock out of Trump Tower. Sater's father, Mikhail, had just been indicted for fraud and racketeering by U.S. district attorney *Lynch* and received two years on probation as a sentence. *Mikhail Sater* reported directly to *Semion Mogilevich*, the Ukrainian-born Russian organized crime boss. In the indictment, Lynch accidentally revealed that Felix Sater was now cooperating with the FBI.

Arif (as a donor) and Sater (a member) were also both involved with *Chabad* in Port Washington. So was *Lev Leviev*, 42, a Bokharan

---

[39] On Bayrock, see James S. Henry, "The Curious World of Donald Trump's Private Russian Connections," *The American Interest*, Vol. 12, No. 4 (December 19, 2016).

Jew from Uzbekistan, a wealthy diamond merchant, who helped Putin create a Federation of Jewish Communities of Russia in 1999. Leviev met oligarchs *Boris Berezovsky* and *Roman Abramovitch* in 1992, and four years later, he founded his own company, Africa Israel Investments, to run his diamond business. Leviev's assistant *Rotem Rosen* then married the daughter of another Bayrock and Chabad figure, *Tamir Sapir*. Donald Trump hosted Rotem Rosen's and Zina Sapir's wedding at Mar-a-Lago in December 2007. Trump's attorney, *Michael Cohen*, was also linked to Chabad, as was Trump's son-in-law *Jared Kushner*, an Orthodox Jew whose family had roots in Belarus.

Jared Kushner attended Harvard College, graduated in 2003 and was elected president of the local Chabad House on campus. Rumors were that his father purchased Jared's admission to Harvard. His grandparents escaped the Holocaust in Belarus during World War II, bought up 4,000 New Jersey apartments and made Jared's father, Charles, very rich. By 2008. Jared was CEO of the Kushner Companies, based in Florham Park, NJ. Jared married Trump's daughter Ivanka in 2009. She converted to Judaism. When the Kushner family with their two children settled in Washington D.C. in 2017, they promptly joined The SHUL, a synagogue run by Chabad whose members include former U.S. Senator Joe Lieberman of Connecticut. (Coincidentally, Chelsea Clinton's husband, Marc Mezvinsky, was also a member of Chabad.) Kushner was also a major realtor in the New York area. In 2007, his company purchased 666 Fifth Avenue, a 41-story office building, for $1.8 billion, the most expensive deal in Manhattan real estate history. And Ivanka became best friends for a time with *Dasha Zhukova*, then wife of Russian oligarch *Roman Abramovich*.

In the meantime, *Charles Kushner* was indicted on 18 counts of *tax evasion*, *illegal campaign contributions*, and *witness tampering* in 2005. Kushner also hired a prostitute to blackmail his brother-in-law, who planned to testify against Kushner in court.[40] Sentenced to two years

---

[40] Michael Wolff, *Fire and Fury. Inside the Trump White House* (NY: Henry Holt, 2018), 31.

in prison, Kushner served 14 months and was released in August 2006. The Kushner family and Trump never forgave New Jersey Governor Chris Christie for allowing Kushner to serve out his jail time. Ivanka convinced her father not to consider Christie for any federal office.

Jared Kushner in 2008, CEO of the Kushner Companies.

The Kushner family was also close to *Beny Steinmetz*, an Israeli-born French billionaire who got rich on real estate and diamond mining in the former Belgian colony of Katanga. In 2012, the Steinmetz Diamond Group partnered with Jared Kushner to purchase $188 million worth of land in Manhattan and New Jersey. Steinmetz was then under investigation by the U.S. Department of Justice. His Scorpio company owned real estate in Russia, Kazakhstan, and eastern Europe. He was a co-founder with William Browder of Hermitage Capital. The FBI investigated Steinmetz for his mining bribes in Guinea, but a RICO lawsuit was dismissed in November 2015. A year later, Steinmetz was arrested on bribery and money laundering charges. In August 2017, Israeli and Swiss authorities arrested him again for fraud, bribery, obstruction of justice, and money laundering.

Meanwhile, in February 2001, FBI mole Robert Hanssen was arrested as a Soviet spy. Russia and the U.S. each expelled 50 diplomats in response. In June, President George W. Bush and Putin met for the first time at a castle outside the capital of Slovenia, Ljubljana, in the former Yugoslavia.

On September 11, 2001, two hijacked airliners shattered the world of New York City. Osama bin Laden's Al Qaeda attack destroyed the twin towers of the World Trade Center and killed thousands of people. Vladimir Putin, Boris Yeltsin's picked successor as president of Russia, visited the George W. Bush White House and ground zero in Manhattan two months later. Loretta Lynch by now had left government service for private practice with the law firm of Hogan & Hartson. Mayor Rudy Giuliani had become "America's mayor" for his decisive handling of the 9/11 disaster and allegedly moved to shut down Italian mafias and inadvertently allow Russian organized crime to flourish. But American faith in both the FBI and CIA was weakened. How could this massive failure of U.S. intelligence have happened?

In the final months of 2001, the U.S. government signed secret agreements with Uzbekistan and Kyrgyzstan to station U.S. troops, aircraft, and support systems in their countries in order to hunt down bin Laden and conduct operations in neighboring Afghanistan in the caves and mountains of Tora Bora directed against Al Qaeda.

Enter *James Comey*. From January 2002 until December 2003, James Comey, 42, was U.S. Attorney for the Southern District of NY. He then worked as U.S. Deputy Attorney General in Washington DC until August 2005. Appointed FBI director by President Barak Obama in 2013, Comey had attended William and Mary College (B.A., 1982), and the U. of Chicago Law School (J.D., 1985). In May 2017, Trump fired Comey as FBI director. Comey obviously knew much too much about Trump, the Russians, and the FBI over a 15-year period.

By 2003, the Bayrock offices were located in Trump Tower. A year later, Bayrock received millions in equity contributions from Arif's brother in Russia, who had access to cash accounts in a chromium refinery in Kazakhstan. Tevfik Arif hired Felix Sater to manage the company, along with *Jody Kriss* as financial COO and attorney *Michael Ejekam* as legal counsel. Sater and Trump may have met for the first time that year. At any rate, the two men made and lost money together for over a decade while Sater was employed by

Trump, who claimed not to remember who his decade-long partner and employee was.[41]

Salvatore Lauria published his gangland memoir *The Scorpion and the Frog* that year. Lauria wrote about Felix Sater under the cryptonym "Lex Tersa." Lauria mentioned Trump on several occasions, primarily because Lauria lived in a Trump penthouse apartment at 40 Wall St.

Bayrock by 2005 had become a complex set of companies designed to get money out of Russia and into Trump's hands. The FL Group was formed for investment as an Icelandic hedge fund (restructured in 2009 as Stodir). Putin and other Russians funded the company, which signed a property agreement with Bayrock and Trump (Trump himself signed). Putin's contacts with Icelandic and Finnish banks went back to his days licensing foreign trade from the St. Petersburg mayor's office in the early 1990s. Salvatore Lauria (by now a convicted felon and FBI informant) brokered $150 million invested by FL to put cash into TrumpSoHo. The FL-Bayrock tax partnership was a sham to evade taxes and launder money. Trump benefitted indirectly because Bayrock kept millions in unpaid taxes and thus evaded $120 million in taxes and liabilities. Trump SoHo became one of five lower-tier companies at the bottom of the Bayrock system. (See Appendix.)

Tamir Sapir and Felix Sater

Trump partnered at this time with *Arif*, a Kazkh billionaire, and Sater, a known Russian gangster, to build TrumpSoHo, a Trump-branded condominium and hotel financed as usual by others' money. In addition to Bayrock, Sater marketed the Trump brand around the U.S. by selling hotel licensing deals through the FL Group in Florida, Arizona, and New York. Trump's second "development partner" with Bayrock was the Sapir Organization of Georgian businessman *Tamir*

---

[41] On the tangled history of Bayrock, see Kriss et. Al. v. Bayrock Group LLC et.al, Southern District of New York, 1:13-cv-03905; Kriss v. Bayrock Group, LLC, U.S. District Court, Southern District of NewYork, No. 10 civ. 3959 (LGS)(FM), February 1, 2016. The 212-page record for State of N.Y. v. Bayrock Group LLC, case index 1010478/2015 was filed under seal but is now available on line. A chart of Bayrock and Trump-owned companies is on page 6. See my appendix.

Sapir, another Jewish member of Chabad. Together Trump and Sapir contemplated a fantasy world of Trump-branded hotels in Moscow, Kiev, Warsaw, and Istanbul.

Arif had promoted Felix Sater to help run Bayrock in 2002. Arif knew only that Sater was born in Russia and emigrated with his family at age eight to Brighton Beach, where his father was a major figure in the Russian mafia. Both Arif and Sater ultimately served as informants to the FBI on Russian mafia doings in Manhattan and Moscow. When Trump and his family visited Moscow in 2006, Sater says he escorted Trump's adult children around the city. It is unclear what Trump knew at this time: that Sater had served a year's jail time for assault in the barroom brawl, been indicted in 1998 on criminal charges of stock fraud and racketeering, and was an FBI informant. But Sater allegedly had grandiose plans: He wanted to run joint Russian and Italian mafia operations out of Trump's building at 40 Wall St., where Sater lived.

Russian cafeteria in Brighton Beach

In addition to the FBI, Sater soon was a valued informant for the CIA on the Eurasian mafia and the arms black market in Afghanistan. Around 1998, he offered to purchase 10 Russian war-surplus Stinger missiles (shoulder-fired) on the black market for $300,000 each and then sell them to his CIA handlers for $3 million each to keep them out of the hands of Osama bin Laden. In return, Sater's stock fraud indictment would be delayed for a decade. Sater was a protected witness.[42]

We know that Sater worked for Donald Trump from 2003 to 2008 on various Trump licensing deals nationwide, from New York to Fort Lauderdale. He had Trump Tower offices, telephones, e-mail, and business cards with Trump organizations. Sater once boasted he could build a Trump Tower anywhere because of his personal relationship with Donald J. Trump. In 2005, Trump signed an exclusive agreement with Bayrock to license Trump buildings in Russia. Sater recommended a number of sites, including the old Sacco and Vanzetti pencil factory outside Moscow managed by American entrepreneur (and Soviet trade agent) Armand Hammer in the 1920s. But Trump failed to build anything in Russia and claimed he could barely remember who Felix Sater was.

Trump's forgetfulness was always selective. Sater was later involved in the 2017 Russian-Ukrainian peace agreement approach to Michael Flynn through Trump's attorney, Michael Cohen, another Chabad member and old friend of Sater. Trump naturally claimed again barely to know Sater, although he had done business with Sater for years and the Bayrock offices were two floors below him in Trump Tower. In addition, Sater had lived in Trump Tower (Floor 24) ever since he got out of prison in the mid-1990s. He was a significant, if forgettable, friend and employee of Donald J. Trump for two decades.

But the money did flow in from Russia. In 2004, Bayrock received millions of dollars in equity contributions from Arif's brother in Russia, who had access to cash accounts for a chromium refinery in Kazakhstan. A year later, Trump married *Melania Knauss*, his third wife, a model from Slovenia, part of the former Yugoslavia that became independent in 1990 and later joined NATO. Melania moved to New York in 1996 and met Trump in 1998. After their first child was born, in 2006, Trump immediately began affairs with porn star Stormy Daniels (Stephanie Clifford) and Playmate Karen McDougal. Sum-

---

[42] On February 10, 2018, the Second Circuit of Appeals unsealed the court dockets, briefings and records for Sater's 1998 conviction for running a pump and dump stock fraud scheme. See Case 11-479, Document 115, 02/09/2018, U.S. Court of Appeals for the Second Circuit.

mer Zervos, an *Apprentice* contestant, later claimed Trump harassed her sexually at about the same time.

Florida investors put up millions of dollars in 2005 for one of the Trump-Sater projects, Trump Tower Tampa. By 2007, they discovered it was a sham project never to be constructed.

In 2006, Trump announced the imminent TrumpSoHo project on his TV program, *The Apprentice*, which had debuted in 2004 and made Trump a star. The Trump-Bayrock partnership became more profitable. Trump never mentioned Bayrock, nor did he mention that the hotel would be partly financed by Tamir Sapir, the Chabad real estate mogul from Soviet Georgia, his son Alex, and his son-in-law *Rotem Rosen*. But in fact, TrumpSoHo was simply a convenient cover for a series of Trump-branded hotels spread from New York and Florida to Arizona, and for moving Trump funds from shelter to shelter. Behind the alleged fraud and tax evasion lay money laundering. To put it briefly, Bayrock was a tax evasion scheme to hide Trump hotels in New York, Florida, and Arizona as third-tier subsidiaries in a much larger corporation.

In September 2007, Trump publicly launched TrumpSoHo with Arif and Sater by his side, along with his children—Donald, Jr., Eric, and Ivanka. The 46-story hotel-condominium complex was to be finished by 2010. A December 2007 article by Charles Bagli in the *NY Times* revealed Felix Sater's criminal past, but not his ongoing relationship with the FBI and CIA.[43] The outed Sater left the U.S. for a year or two and worked in Russia for the Mirax Group of real estate developers. On September 14, two shell companies, Bayrock B.V. and KazBay B.V., signed an agreement with Helvetia Capital (nominally Khrapunov's wife); on September 25, Bayrock B.V. transferred $740,000 into a KazBay account, but in the end, some $1.4 million simply vanished into the money laundromat. Donald Trump Jr. boasted in September 2008 that "we see a lot of money pouring in from Russia."[44] In 2011, Ivanka and Eric were nearly charged with

---

[43] Charles V. Bagli, "Real Estate Executive with Hand in Trump Projects Rose from Tangled Past," *New York Times*, December 17, 2007.

[44] Hazel Heyer of eTurboNews, a trade journal, quoted young Trump in her report on his speech on September 15, 2008.

crimes in connection with Trump SoHo until their father's attorney, Marc Kasowitz, gave a substantial political donation to Manhattan district attorney Cyrus Vance. The SoHo case quietly vanished from sight.

Trump's attorney Marc Kasowitz promptly sued Timothy O'Brien and Time-Warner for defamation in New Jersey Superior Court for O'Brien's 2008 "tell all" book, *Trump Nation: The Art of Being the Donald*. In a December 19 deposition, Trump claimed he barely knew Felix Sater as an employee of Bayrock, a company Trump did not own.

> "Q: Put aside Bayrock. Other than this situation, have you ever before associated with individuals you knew were associated with organized crime?
> "A: Not that I know of."[45]

Many knew differently. In 2011, Trump lost his defamation case against O'Brien.

Eric Trump, Tevfik Arif, Donald Trump Jr., Ivanka Trump, Donald J. Trump, Tamir Sapir, Alex Sapir, Julius Schwarz, announcing Trump-SoHo construction project with Bayrock.

Credit: Wireimage, 2007.

---

[45] December 19, 2007 deposition, Donald Trump v. Timothy O'Brien, Time-Warner, NJ Superior Court, Case CAM-L-545-06, 414. Trump lost this defamation case in 2011.

TrumpSoHo was planned as a $370 million complex that could generate $227 million in profits. Trump owed $560 million for construction costs, but money kept arriving "magically" from Russia. In 2008, Felix Sater left Bayrock (which now had 12 subsidiary holding companies). In an email to an investor, Sater crowed that "Donald is happy with me." *Jody Kriss* also resigned from Bayrock as COO, complaining that Trump now owed him $7 million and that Bayrock profits seem to be going to Russia via the FL Group in Iceland. Or to Donald Trump. Who knew.

Racketeering
In any event, Kriss sued Sater, Arif, Trump, and Bayrock in Delaware. In December 2016, a federal judge in New York ruled that Kriss's lawsuit could proceed as a RICO *racketeering* case. Kriss considered both Trump and Sater to be compulsive liars as well as practiced criminals and racketeers.

Bernie Madoff's arrest in late 2009 suggested caution. The well-known financier had bilked thousands of wealthy Jewish investors out of more than $60 billion in one of the greatest Ponzi schemes ever. After pleading guilty to 11 charges of fraud (securities, mail, and wire), perjury, money laundering, and false advertising, Madoff himself received a jail sentence of 150 years. Many of his victims lost everything in an affinity fraud scandal that suggested great care in marketing an investment scheme to older and vulnerable investors. Trump promptly let the media know he had reduced his Mar-a-Lago membership fee for Madoff's victims in the Miami and Palm Beach area.

On October 3, 2009, Felix Sater was finally sentenced to probation and a (suspended) $25,000 fine for his decade-old racketeering indictment. The sentence was lenient and long overdue. More important for the U.S. government, Sater's secret identity as an FBI and CIA informant since 1998 was protected. In 2010, Sater donated $100,000 to Chabad House in Port Washington and was chosen its Man of the Year in 2014.

Also in 2010, police in Istanbul raided the luxury yacht of Tefvik Arif and charged him in a Turkish court with smuggling underage girls into Turkey for prostitution purposes. The yacht was full of them. Tamir Sapir was also implicated. So was the Kazakh trio of *Alexander Mashkevich, Patokh Chodiev*, and *Alijan Ibragimov*. Trump in the meantime was pursuing the possibility of a Trump Plaza luxury hotel in Riga, Latvia, with the billionaire music promoter *Igor Krutoy*. Ivanka Kushner discussed the possibilities with Krutoy in Trump Tower in June 2011. Enthusiasm waned, however, when word spread that Latvian authorities and the FBI were investigating Krutoy on corruption charges linked to organized crime.

Sater continued to work for Trump out of Trump Tower with a business card ("Senior Adviser to Donald Trump"), telephone, computer, and offices. On February 10, 2011, the U.S. Court of Appeals, 2nd circuit in New York instructed attorney *Fred Oberlander* not to inform Congress in any way of what he knew about Sater. *Richard Lerner* was Oberlander's attorney for this case. Jody Kriss meanwhile commenced a legal campaign against Bayrock that would last into 2015.

At the same time, *Loretta Lynch* returned as U.S. attorney for EDNY. She had worked with Sater since 1998 and was well aware of the odd arrangements with Trump Tower. *Paul Clement*, Solicitor General, prepared a civil racketeering RICO suit against Sater. But Sater was much too important for his cover to be blown. Both eastern and southern New York federal attorneys issued restraining orders sealing and barring dissemination of any previously sealed Sater documents.

TrumpSoHo was a case of *fraud*. On March 17, 2011, Loretta Lynch ruled that the court should "unseal those dockets and maintain the rest under seal." On May 20, Trump settled a lawsuit against him and Ivanka Trump for defrauding Trump SoHo purchasers of condos "without prejudice." The indictment charged "undisclosed involvement of convicted felons" and questionable Russian and Kazakh financiers, therefore *fraud* and *false advertising*. Fewer than 30 percent of units had been sold by 2009. To settle, depositors received $2.84 million, or 90 percent of their $3.16 million deposits back. Trump continued to receive his 18 percent of profits of TrumpSoHo until the foreclosure. The lawsuit against the Trumps was filed under federal

RICO, Racketeer Influenced and Corrupt Practices Act, terms. After settlement, TrumpSoHo was closed as a criminal case. Trump and Felix Sater knew too much, and the FBI offered protection. Court records were sealed.

Meanwhile, the new 70-story Trump International Hotel in Panama City, Panama, was becoming a money laundry, safe house, and investment opportunity for organized crime, notably Columbian drug dealers and Russian mafia types whose names never appeared in the shell company documents for rentals or purchases. When CNN investigated the hotel a few years later, they found only empty rooms and darkened hallways with very few signs of human habitation. In 2017, *Orestes Fintiklis*, 39, an Oxford-educated Cypriot financier, purchased 202 of 369 hotel units now managed by Donald Trump Jr. and his brother Eric, then sued the Trump Organization for its "abysmal" management of the hotel it did not own.[46] Money from Cyprus, perhaps Russian, underwrote the Trump brand and Trump management until Fintiklis and his colleagues, with Panamanian government support, forced the Trumps out and removed their brand name from the hotel in March 2018.

Closing down Bayrock was in the interest of all concerned. Trump settled a complex racketeering and fraud case he was probably going to lose. Sater maintained his "don't ask, don't tell" relationship with the FBI and CIA that kept Sater out of jail. The U.S. government purchased silence from men who knew much too much about Donald Trump, 9/11, al Qaeda, and Eurasian organized crime.

Viktor Khrapunov and the Loot of Kazakhstan

Bayrock demonstrated clearly that Eurasian organized crime was more than the Russian mafia, had significant interests in the New York real estate market, and was a sustainable means of getting money to Trump in order to keep his operations going. The key players in Bayrock were not only Russians and Chabad Jews, but Kazakhs.

Viktor Khrapunov left Kazakhstan for Switzerland in 2008 with a reported $4 billion in stolen assets from his time as mayor of Al-

---

[46] On the Trump International Hotel, see the *New York Times*, March 4, 2018, 1, 4.

maty (1997-2007). Khrapunov promptly set up his money laundering operations under the name Helvetic Capital SA. He arrived in Geneva in August with 18 tons of looted valuables, cash and antiques from Kazakhstan in his airplane. Naturally, he denied any criminal activity.

But in May 2011, the government of Kazakhstan filed two criminal cases against Khrapunov: *abuse of power* and *fraud* for personal gain. An Interpol warrant for his arrest was duly issued. He allegedly looted some $4 billion worth of valuables and money from Kazakhstan. Now where could he hide it?

The enterprising Felix Sater now went to work for *Viktor Khrapunov*. Former employees of Bayrock testified in 2012 that the company was a monument to corrupt *money laundering* and *tax evasion* via a Delaware corporation through FL Iceland to Russia. The "Delaware Tax Laundromat" was intended to evade U.S. taxes. *Jody Kriss* now sued Bayrock for $1 billion in damages.

Bayrock, threatened with foreclosure, finally closed down in 2013 and was sold to its shell companies controlled by *Viktor Khrapunov*, for a nominal $3.1 million. Khrapunov's son, Ilyas, was involved; so was his daughter, Elvira Kudryashova, who lived in California. In April, Khrapunov created three new companies to launder Bayrock money: Soho3310, Soho3311, and Soho3213. He also paid $3.1 million for his own apartments in TrumpSoHo.

Meanwhile, Felix Sater and another Bayrock employee, *Daniel Ridloff*, extended their Kazakhstan-Russia-U.S. money laundering activities for Trump to an Ohio Tri-County Mall near Cincinnati. When the mall was sold off, a Swiss financier accused Sater and Ridloff of absconding with $43 million. After much litigation, the case was settled out of court. Sater and Ridloff made about $20 million between them from the scam.

Jody Kriss filed another lawsuit against Bayrock on May 10, 2013, in the Southern District of New York. The suit contended a billion dollars in *fraud* because of the "illegal concealment of Felix Sater's 1998 $40 million federal racketeering conviction and subsequent 2009 sentencing."[47] Kriss asked for relief. Sater himself admitted to participating in the operation of a "pump-and-dump" stock fraud, along with members of the Russian and Mafia organized crime that had defrauded many senior citizen investors through Bayrock.

Sater, Arif, and *Julius Schwarz*, the Bayrock executive vice president and general counsel, had managed to skim off more than $27 million in a massive "mob owned and operated business" that disguised the sale of partnership interests in a tax evasion and money laundering scheme. They failed to report Bayrock income of $50-100 million that cost the State of New York some $7-21 million in uncollected taxes. Finally, *Preet Bharara*, U.S. attorney for the Southern District of New York, removed the 2013 Bayrock case to federal court on June 7.[48]

Jody Kriss

In 2014, Tamir Sapir died at the age of 67. Russian occupation of the Crimea and Eastern Ukraine led Schwarzman and Blackstone to give up on Russian investments and avoid entanglements with Eurasian organized crime. And Chabad House in Port Washington named

[47] U.S. v. Felix Sater, Criminal Docket No. 98, CR 1101 (ILG), 2009.

[48] State of New York v. Bayrock Group LLC, 4, 18.

Felix Sater its "man of the year," thanks in part to Arif's financial support. Sater's James Bond-like deeds for the FBI and CIA were alluded to, and celebrated at a banquet, but never specified.

In March, the U.S. Congress levied sanctions against Russian individuals and companies for Russian occupation of Crimea and Eastern Ukraine. Salvatore Lauria filed a $5 million lawsuit against Jody Kriss for attempting to kill ("whack") Lauria in July 2012 by means of a mafia beating at a Brooklyn restaurant. Kriss hated Lauria because Lauria had taken the entire Bayrock commission for himself in an $85 million real estate deal with the FL Group of Iceland. There was no honor among thieves.

Tax Fraud, Extortion, Bayrock and the Trumps

In January 2015, at her Senate confirmation hearing for the post of U.S. Attorney General, *Loretta Lynch* explained to curious Senators that Felix Sater's court records were sealed because for more than a decade Sater was "providing information crucial to national security and the conviction of over 20 individuals, including those responsible for committing massive financial fraud and members of La Cosa Nostra." On February 17, Sater criticized Lynch and referred to her "contemptuous seven-year legal battle" over sealing the documents in his case. Jody Kriss's lawyers Oberlander and Lerner were ordered to return all documents taken from Sater and Bayrock or risk going to prison. They tried to use the Sater case to derail President Obama's nomination of Lynch as U.S. attorney general, but the U.S. Senate confirmed Lynch's appointment on April 23.

In May 2015, Trump's son-in-law, Jared Kushner, purchased a $295 million share in the old *New York Times* building on West 43rd St. from none other than Vladimir Putin's old friend, *Lev Leviev*. Leviev's Africa Israel Investments company was the owner of the building. And both men were members of Chabad. Kushner's money came from a Deutsche Bank loan.

Trump claims not to remember Sater or Arif or Bayrock. Yet on October 13, 2015, Trump signed a letter of intent for a Trump Tower in Moscow drafted by Felix Sater and reviewed by Trump's attorney,

Michael Cohen. Sater also wrote Cohen: "Buddy our boy can become president of the USA and we can engineer it. I will get all of Putin's team to buy in on this. I will manage this process."[49] Sater added that it would be "pretty cool to get a USA president elected." Thus did Felix Sater help organize the Trump campaign.

In 2016, Trump appointed *Steven Schwarzman* to his presidential Strategic and Policy Forum. On October 11, Felix Sater sued Bayrock claiming that from 2008 to 2015, Jody Kriss had created a $250 million *tax-fraud extortion* campaign against Bayrock by filing five separate lawsuits. Kriss also sued Trump and his children. Kriss accused the new U.S. Attorney General *Loretta Lynch* of collaboration with Sater to protect Sater as an FBI informant. It was a wilderness of mirrors and doublespeak involving the Trumps, Russian mafia, and Kazakhs. But noone was talking.

In February 2017, Kriss and his attorney Ejekam filed motions opposing Bayrock's attempt to silence them and end prolonged litigation. In April, Robert Amsterdam, Mikhail Khodorkovsky's attorney in Canada, stated "the FBI has an informer who was once part of the Trump organization" and may be protecting a source. Felix Sater was the most likely FBI informer working for Trump and a "cooperating witness" for the FBI. Both Sater and Trump had knowledge from the Bayrock experience and their Chabad connections that could reveal secrets neither the FBI nor the CIA wished known. And Trump's connections to the FBI went back at least to 1981.

By the end of 2017, TrumpSoHo had closed its restaurant and removed the Trump name from the entire enterprise. Both Jared Kushner and Felix Sater were by then targets of the special Russia prosecutor, Robert Mueller. For U.S. President Donald J. Trump, everything involving Trump SoHo disappeared down the memory hole. Except the money.

"Greed," Felix Sater cheerfully reminded the media in 2018, "is my go-to weapon."

---

[49] Felix Sater email to Michael Cohen, November 3, 2015.

Paul Manafort turning himself into the FBI in 2017.

5. PAUL MANAFORT, FOREIGN AGENT

Manafort! He's been a Russian stooge for 15 years.
—Victoria Nuland, former U.S. assistant Secretary of State, 2016

The Orange Revolution in Ukraine in 2004 was a hopeful sign that the newly independent nation might align itself with the West and perhaps even join NATO, a nightmare scenario for Putin and the Russians. Kiev and Ukraine were the birthplace of Moscow and Russia since the tenth century. Slavic Ukraine also developed ties with Catholic Poland and the Vatican over the years. The Baltic nations (Estonia, Latvia, Lithuania), once part of the Kingdom of Poland-Lithuania, had just joined NATO and the European Union them-selves. Putin had no desire to see Ukraine become a western dagger pointed at the heart of Russia.

In July, 2004, Putin flew to Crimea to meet with *Viktor Yanukovych,* Ukrainian prime minister since 2002 and Putin's favored candidate in the upcoming October 31 presidential elections. At Yalta, Putin warned Yanukovych and former President Kuchma of the dangers of Ukraine joining either NATO or the European Union. The politicians agreed to create a new energy company, RosUkrEnergo, half owned by Gazprom. The non-Gazprom half was owned by a shadow company based in Austria, Raiffeisen International, that included mobsters *Semion Mogilevich* and *Dmytro Firtash*. Putin also agreed to pay half of the pro-Russian Yanukovych's campaign expenses in the coming election. Mogilevich and Firtash agreed to keep the gas piplines to Europe in operation.

On October 31, *Viktor Yushchenko* barely beat Yanukovych at the polls (39.87 percent to 39.32 percent), with 20 other minor candidates running behind them. But Yanukovych won the second-round runoff despite widespread allegations of voter fraud. Austrian doctors declared that Yushchenko had been recently poisoned by dioxin. In a second runoff election in December, Yushchenko beat Yanukovych (52 percent to 44 percent). The Orange Revolution election appeared in Russia to be a defeat. In most of Ukraine, the election looked like a vote for independence from Russia and for closer ties to Europe. Putin fumed.

In December 2005, Gazprom shut off the natural gas pipeline through Ukraine to Europe. The winter energy crisis was ultimately resolved and Gazprom reaped the continuing profits of selling gas to Ukraine and Europe. The defeated Yanukovych now began his political comeback and makeover with the help of an American Republican Party consultant, Paul Manafort.

Working for Yanukovych and Deripaska

Manafort emerged in 2006 as an adviser to *Viktor Yanukovych* and *Oleg Deripaska*, a Ukrainian billionaire and friend of Putin.[50] In New York, Manafort also purchased a condo on Floor 43 of Trump Tower for $3.7 million. His client, Oleg Deripaska, was less fortunate, barred from entering U.S. because of his ties to Russian organized crime. But Manafort would become a crucial link between Trump and Putin, a U.S. Russian agent working in Ukraine for Moscow's ruler.

At 57, with a Georgetown University law degree, Manafort was an attorney, lobbyist and wheeler-dealer on the payroll of authoritarian

---

[50] On Manafort as the agent of Yanukovych and Putin, see Harding, *Collusion*, 142-72.

rulers like Ferdinand Marcos and Jonas Savimbi, known for their misdeeds in the Phillipines and Angola respectively. Manafort's rumored links with Russian arms dealers, oligarchs, and organized crime proved less important than his friendship with Donald Trump, beginning in the early 1980s when Sen. Joseph McCarthy's and Trump family attorney, *Roy Cohn*, introduced the two men. In 2016, Manafort organized and then abandoned Trump's apparently sinking presidential campaign because Manafort's financial ties to Ukraine, Russia, and Eurasian organized crime had become a major Trump campaign liability.

Manafort's grandfather, James, moved to Connecticut from Sicily in 1919 and founded the New Britain House-Wrecking Company, now Manafort Brothers.[51] In April 2014, the company paid $2.4 million in fines for making false statements about alleged fraud in public works projects in Connecticut. Paul Manafort's father was once mayor of New Britain and a leader of the Italo-American community there. Now Ukrainian-Americans were demonstrating on Paul Manafort Avenue against Russia's occupation of eastern Ukraine.

In the 1980s, Paul Manafort joined *Lee Atwater's* D.C. law firm known as the "torturer's lobby" for its work on behalf of murderous dictators everywhere. Manafort helped repackage dictators as freedom fighters—for a large fee. He befriended the arms dealer Abdul Rahman Al Assir, the one-time brother-in-law of Adnan Kashoggi. He also stage-managed GOP convention operations for presidential candidates Ford, Reagan, Dole, and George H.W. Bush. His attorney was William Sessions, the Republican FBI director fired by the Clinton administration for conflict of interest violations. His aide was a young staffer named *Rick Gates*. In addition, Manafort helped run a "long con" to convert resentful white workers into GOP voters that reached its climax in the Trump run to the U.S. presidency.

Manafort discovered Ukrainian politics in 2005 when he advised *Rinat Akhmatov*, another billionaire coal oligarch from the Donbas in Eastern Ukraine and a supporter of Yanukovych. Akhmatov for years had defended himself against charges he was involved in the "Donetsk

---

[51] See Franklin Foer, "The Plot against America. Paul Manafort and the Fall of Washington," *The Atlantic*, March 2018.

mafia" of his Tatar mentor *Akhat Bragin*, a network of organized crime in an area of Ukraine dominated by Russians. Yanukovych had the reputation of being tied to the mafia since 1967, when he spent three years in prison for robbery and assault. Raised in the Donbas area of Ukraine, he spoke Russian better than Ukrainian. Manafort helped Yanukovych clean up his political act.

Manafort probably first met Yanukovych in summer 2005 in Karlo Vary (Carlsbad), a Czech resort town populated by wealthy Russians, including Russian mafia, who owned most property in town. Akhmatov, by then the wealthiest man in Ukraine (he lives at One Hyde Park in London), and a longtime friend of Yanukovych and Putin, set up the meeting. U.S. ambassador to Ukraine *William Taylor* warned Manafort personally in 2006 that steering Ukraine away from Europe toward Russia was in direct opposition to U.S. interests. According to the U.S. State Department, Manafort was trying to give an extreme makeover to Yanukovych and his Party of Regions, which the Department considered a haven for Donetsk-based mobsters.

Manafort also did business with *Oleg Deripaska*, the oligarch aluminum king who also managed the funds of the organized crime Izmailovskaya gang from Moscow. Organized in the mid 1980s, the gang engaged in robberies and protection shakedowns, feuded with Chechen gangs and used a network of casinos for money laundering.

Manafort's liaison with Deripaska was *Konstantin Kilimnik*, a Ukrainian who ran Manafort's office in Kiev until 2014. Kilimnik attended a GRU military intelligence training university for foreign languages in the late 1980s. He met Manafort twice in New York while Manafort was running Trump's campaign (in May and August 2016). Allegedly tied to the FSB and Russian intelligence, Kilimnik helped Manafort violate a court order following his indictment (for lying to the FBI and money laundering) in 2017 by co-authoring an editorial regarding Russian behavior in Ukraine. In December 2006, Manafort brought Yanukovych to Washington D.C. to meet Vice President Dick Cheney and other luminaries. The FBI received complaints that Manafort was behaving like an unregistered agent, which he was.

In 2007, Yanukovych's Party of Regions made the first of two payments to Manafort totaling $1.2 million. Manafort received a wire transfer of $455,000 that migrated from Kiev to Belize shell companies, then on to Manafort's Virginia bank account. A second payment on October 14, 2009, was for $750,000. By 2014, Manafort had received over $17 million from Russian sources in Ukraine for strategic counsel and advice. He was a Russian agent unregistered in the U.S. A vengeful Oleg Deripaska claimed Manafort was running a real estate scam and owed him the $17 million.

As a result, Yanukovych won the presidency of Ukraine in February 2010, jailed many opposition leaders (including his opponent, *Iulia Tymoshenko*), and was forced from power in February 2014, when he fled to Russia (Rostov-on-Don). He stole an estimated $100 billion in four years and took $32 billion with him when he fled Ukraine in a helicopter.

As of 2016, Paul Manafort had not yet registered in the U.S. as a Russian or Ukrainian foreign agent, nor did he show any signs of doing so. Then, in June 2017, Manafort belatedly declared himself to the Justice Department as a FARA-registered foreign agent of Ukraine. He also established numerous offshore companies for money laundering, including his Global Endeavor company in St. Vincent and the Grenadines and Lucicle Consultants in Cyprus. Together with his aide, Rick Gates, Manafort managed to move millions of dollars into the U.S. through untraceable bank accounts and companies, many of them through Cyprus, the money laundering capital of Europe.

Dmytro Firtash, Bribery and Racketeering

Dmytro Firtash was a billionaire owner of Ukrainian metal companies. In 2007, Firtash, 42, formed Group DF, a conglomerate of chemical, real estate, and energy companies. He controlled RosUkrEnergo and the titanium industry of Ukraine, among many other industries. Titanium was a critical lightweight metal highly prized in medicine and the aircraft industry. Group DF was registered in the British Virgin Islands and linked to Manafort through his global consulting operations. Firtash's Group DF conglomerate also owned Spadi Trading company in Cyprus, a favorite safe haven for Russian and Ukrainian capital assets. After 2001, Firtash also ran Highrock Holding Company, a Cyprus front for the Mogilevich crime family.

A year later, Paul Manafort got involved in a $895 million project in Manhattan to turn the decrepit Drake Hotel into an upscale Bulgari Tower with Firtash's financial support. Firtash and Manafort organized CMZ Ventures in New York (with Arthur Cohen and Brad Zackson, hence the acronym; Zackson worked for Donald Trump.) Firtash put up $25 million for the start-up in 2008. Manafort and his CMZ partners got $1.5 million for managing Firtash's money. The FBI at the time was investigating Firtash, co-owner of RusUkrEnergo, for bribery in connection with procuring titanium in India for Boeing Aircraft in Chicago. The court in Chicago indicted Firtash on bribery and racketeering charges in October 2013, and Austria arrested him a few months later in Vienna. He currently awaits extradition to the U.S. and Spain. The Bulgari Tower project fell through and the $25 million disappeared from view.[52]

Manafort claims to have done no business with Firtash. But Manafort and his aide, Rick Gates, did have dealings with Oleg Deripaska, another billionaire ally of Yanukovych, whose Surf Island company paid out $7.35 million in "management fees" to Manafort and his partners in a Cayman Islands investment fund of $18.9 million using the Bank of Cyprus, ostensibly for a Black Sea Telecom purchase, but more probably as a tax dodge. Allegedly, Deripaska paid Manafort an annual retainer of $10 million from 2006 through 2009. Manafort visited Cyprus in early 2017 and became entangled in litigation over money, first in the Cayman Islands and then in New York. Rick Gates registered Cypriot shell companies for Manafort to use in money transfers. More important, U.S. officials denied Deripaska permission to enter the country for years because of his apparent ties to the Russian mafia and Eurasian organized crime.

In February 2010, Manafort helped Viktor Yanukovych win the presidential election in Ukraine, defeating *Yulia Timoshenko*, a former prime minister of the Orange Revolution, in a relatively honest elec-

---

[52] On the Firtash case, see Department of Justice, *Justice News*, April 2, 2014.

tion. But Timoshenko was then convicted and jailed for negotiating a second deal with Putin to end another shutoff of Russian natural gas to Ukraine in 2009. Her political enemies locked her up.

In 2011, Yulia Timoshenko filed a lawsuit in Manhattan alleging that Paul Manafort was behind a *racketeering* and *money-laundering* plot to hide $3.5 million in stolen funds in U.S. real estate using his CMZ shell company. Co-defendants were Dmitry Firtash and Semion Mogilevich of RosUkrEnergo, neither of whom could legally enter the U.S. because they were considered members of Eurasian organized crime circles headed by Mogilevich. In May, Firtash purchased the Nadra Bank in Ukraine, which closed two years later. After much litigation, the Timoshenko lawsuit was dismissed in 2015. The lawyer drafting a report for the Ukraine Ministry of Justice, *Alex van der Zwaan*, son-in-law of Alfa Group billionaire *German Khan*, was later (in 2018) indicted for lying to the FBI and the special counsel, Robert Mueller.[53] Van der Zwaan apparently worked for Yanukovych, Manafort and Rick Gates through Skadden, Arps law firm. Manafort and Gates secretly funded the report with four million dollars from an offshore account, probably in Cyprus. Van der Zwaan provided a draft of his report to the Ministry of Justice's public relations firm in advance.

On November 21, 2013, Yanukovych backed out of a negotiated agreement with the European Union under pressure from Vladimir Putin and the Russians. Thousands of Ukrainians rioted in Kiev. On December 17, Yanukovych announced a new deal with Russia whereby Moscow would give Ukraine a cash infusion of $15 billion and Gazprom would cut the price of natural gas from $400 per cubic meter to $268.

On June 20, a Chicago grand jury returned (under seal) an indictment against Dmytro Firtash and five other defendants charged with *racketeering* and *money laundering conspiracy*, plus interstate travel to aid racketeering. Most charges involved bribing Indian officials with $18.5 million since 2006 to procure licenses to mine titanium

---

[53] Van der Zwaan pled guilty on February 20, 2018 to the felony of lying to the FBI and Mueller and was arraigned in the U.S. District Court of DC. Zwaan lied on November 3, 2017, days after Manafort's own indictment.

for use in aircraft construction and medical technology, using 57 fund transfers.[54]

In early 2014, Viktor Yanukovych ordered a crackdown on demonstrators in Maidan Square in Kiev that killed more than 100 people. Victoria Nuland, a U.S. State Department officer, supported regime change in Ukraine and passed out cookies and sandwiches to the demonstrators. On February 22, the parliament in Kiev ousted Yanukovych as president because of his human rights violations and dereliction of duty. When he fled to Rostov, Yanukovych left behind a "black ledger" with 22 entries showing $12.7 million in payments by the Party of Regions to Manafort. Manafort might have gotten the pro-Russian president elected to office, but he failed to engineer competence or justice. That was not the point.

The demise of Yanukovych devastated Manafort. In 2015, he contemplated suicide and considered divorcing his wife. His financial transactions and holdings were under scrutiny. His cash flow was limited. And Ukraine was in turmoil because of Putin's invasion.

Dmitro Firtash, co-owner of RusUkrEnergo

Dmytro Firtash was going down. On March 13, 2014, the Austrian police arrested Firtash in Vienna. He was held pending extradi-

---

[54] On the Firtash case, see Department of Justice, *Justice News*, April 2, 2014, where Firtash was named as "the leader of the enterprise."

tion requests from both Spain and the U.S. Most charges were from the Chicago indictment of June 20, 2013: *conspiracy to commit racketeering* and *money laundering* using international travel.

On March 27, 2014, the U.S. House of Representatives (by a 399-19 vote) and the Senate (on a voice vote) agreed to a $1 billion loan to Ukraine, sanctioned various Russians involved in the invasion of Crimea and Eastern Ukraine, and suggested that future U.S. military aid to Ukraine was possible. On April 28, sanctions were extended to seven more Russian officials, including Igor Sechin of Rosneft, and 17 Russian companies. In July, the U.S. Specially Designated Nationals List (SDN) imposed sanctions, froze U.S. assets, and restricted any business dealings with U.S. citizens and companies for a broad range of Russian individuals and companies. The U.S. imposed further sanctions in December on the Moscow-based VTB Bank with which Trump would negotiate for a Trump Tower in Moscow loan in October 2016, just prior to his election.

"America," tweeted Donald Trump, "is at a great disadvantage. Putin is ex-KGB, Obama is a community organizer. Unfair."[55]

Manafort now turned to Trump. In April 2016, the Trump presidential campaign accepted Paul Manafort as its senior adviser, and Manafort closed down his office in Kiev run by Kilimnik. In July, Manafort through Kilimnik offered to provide Deripaska a private briefing with Trump. By August 14, the *NY Times* reported that Manafort was listed 22 times in Ukrainian ledger books as having received $12.7 million in cash for supporting Russian interests in Ukrainian elections. Two days later, Manafort resigned from the Trump campaign. He had been campaign chair for less than four months.

Since April 2000, the FBI has operated an organized crime task force in Budapest to monitor Eastern Europe. Trial attorney *Lisa Page* was involved in following the money laundering of Dmitry Firtash. (She later worked for special prosecutor Robert Mueller.) The FBI then began investigating Paul Manafort in connection with the Trump campaign's connections with Russia and Ukraine. But Manafort's links to Donald Trump went back nearly 40 years, and Manafort had resided in Trump Tower for a decade. Morover, he had links to Eurasian organized crime that could not be ignored.

In July 2016, Christopher Steele wrote that Manafort was involved in an "extensive conspiracy" between the Trump Campaign and Moscow, "using foreign policy adviser Carter Page and others as intermediaries." Putin was determined to defeat Hillary Clinton and elect Donald Trump, even while he thought Yanukovych was simply another useful "idiot."

On July 26, 2017, the FBI searched Manafort's suburban Virginia home on the grounds of probable cause that a crime had been committed there. Federal indictments of Manafort and Gates followed. In January 2018, Manafort counter-sued the Department of Justice and Special Prosecutor Robert Mueller for exceeding their authority to investigate Russian involvement in the 2016 election. But to add insult to injury, Oleg Deripaska, in January 2018, filed yet another lawsuit against Manafort and Gates in a New York State court, this time for fraud.

Bank of Cyprus, Nicosia

6. CYPRUS AND THE OFFSHORE LAUNDROMATS

*Transaction laundering is serious misconduct—often
criminal. It violates the merchant's agreement with its acquirer,
allows prohibited goods and services to enter the payment system,
and may flout anti-money laundering laws.*
—Dan Frechtling, June 27, 2017

Russian capital fled offshore after 1991. With the collapse of the Soviet Union and its banking system, the Republic of Cyprus began receiving an average of $1 billion of Russian capital outflow *per month* (as of 1994). An estimated 40 thousand Russians were living in Cyprus by 2010. Many more had their own bank accounts there. Russians held a quarter of Cyprus bank deposits and controlled 37 percent of foreign investment in Cyprus, mainly in the Greek sector. Thus, Cyprus became a favorite offshore site for Russian money laundering worldwide.

Money laundering has been a U.S. federal crime since 1986 when Congress passed a "Money Laundering Control Act." The act made it illegal to engage in a financial transaction in criminally derived property; to conceal such a transaction by commercial means; or to transport a "money instrument" internationally to disguise its true ownership.[56] Buying expensive real estate was a common form of concealment, so that many Russians held disguised assets offshore.

In October 1995, U.S. president Bill Clinton addressed the UN and called for a worldwide attack on terrorism, organized crime, drug trafficking, and nuclear smuggling. Many such activities involved money laundering and the island nation of Cyprus, divided for decades into Greek and Turkish sectors.

A month after Clinton's address, a confidential report by Britain's National Crime Squad asserted that Semion Mogilevich had been illegally transferring funds from Britain to Hungary, then to the U.S., then Canada using his YBM company in Pennsylvania as a money-laundering operation.

When Russian émigrés *Lucy Edwards* and *Peter Berlin* opened two bank accounts in Moscow for their employer, the Bank of New York (BONY) in 1996, they were running the London office's East European Division for BONY. Berlin was already suspected of ties to Semion Mogilevich and Russian mafia. Now, he was into money laundering.

In 1998, the U.S. Organized Crime Task Force (FBI, IRS, INS, Customs and State Department) in Philadelphia raided the YBM office in Newtown, Pennsylvania, and claimed it was simply a money laundering shell company for Mogilevich. Jacob Bogatin received a "target letter" from the U.S. Justice Department stating the Task Force had sufficient evidence to indict Bogatin for money laundering. He resigned from the company two days later.

In August 1998, Russian banks suffered a meltdown. Half of the 1,500 banks in Russia were declared insolvent. Mobbed-up banks were caught stealing money from western loans. Bank officials looted their own banks. Central Bank chief *Sergei Dubinin*, like many other Russians, had hidden much of his cash in Cyprus bank accounts. ExxonMobil's CEO Rex Tillerson now began doing deals with Rosneft, the Russian oil and gas company headed by Putin's old Leningrad pal, Igor Sechin.

When Trump World Tower was completed in 1999, one third of its occupants were from Russia, Kazakhstan, and Ukraine. Like

---

[56] See "Money Laundering Control Act of 1986," PL 99-570, U.S. Act of Congress, H.R. 5077, July 22, 1986.

Trump Tower, the new building became a place to store assets from the former Soviet Union. *Edward Nektalov*, a diamond merchant from Uzbekistan, invested Eurasian mob money in the World Tower before being shot to death on Fifth Avenue in 2002. *Anatoly Golubchik* and *Mikhail Sall* joined the many Russian-speaking tenants of Trump's Sunny Isles condo complex in Miami before being convicted of gambling and money laundering.

U.S. authorities in 2000 accused the Bank of New York of money-laundering billions of dollars for Russian and Eurasian organized crime. Wire transfers moved money from Moscow, London and New York to offshore accounts worldwide. Bank officials Lucy Edwards and Peter Berlin subsequently pleaded guilty to money-laundering charges. An estimated $7 billion in Russian monies had been laundered through BONY. The case continued in the courts until BONY finally fired Lucy Edwards for "gross misconduct" on August 28. Berlin then surrendered himself to the FBI.

In the wake of the 9/11 attacks, the FBI set up offices in Budapest, targeting Mogilevich, Berlin, and the Russian mob. *Grant D. Ashley*, FBI assistant director for the criminal investigation division, reported in 2003 that Russian organized crime gangs had transferred $9 billion in assets out of Russia through Russian banks. At the time, the FBI was dealing with more than 200 ongoing cases of Russian and Eurasian money laundering. On November 9, 2005, BONY settled its Russian money laundering lawsuit and agreed to pay $38 million in penalties after a six-year investigation. The bank thus admitted to criminal conduct.

Cyprus joined the EU in 2008 and began to use the Euro currency. The island soon became a major offshore tax haven and money laundering center for Putin and wealthy Russians. As prime minister (2008-2012), Putin was also chair of the VEB bank, wholly owned by the Russian government. Paul Manafort opened at least 15 bank accounts in Cyprus. Five of these accounts exhibited 13 suspicious wire transfers of $3 million in 2012-2013. Donald Trump had two companies registered in the island: Trump Construction Co. LTD and UA Trump International Investments. The Bank of Cyprus became the major laundromat cleaning money moving between New York and Moscow. Dmytro Firtash based his Highrock Holdings shell company in Cyprus.

A Cyprus real estate investment company named Prevezon Holdings (2007), run by *Denis Katsyv*, laundered $230 million for 11 companies. Katsyv's lawyer was *Natalia Veselnitskaya*, the Russian attorney who later lobbied against the Magnitsky Act sanctioning Russians who conspired to murder imprisoned Moscow attorney Sergei Magnitsky. Putin responded by stopping all U.S. adoptions of Russian children. Magnitsky was investigating Prevezon just before he died in prison in 2009. The scheme involved ID theft to file fake tax refunds and hacking into William Browder's Hermitage Capital Management Company, whose accountant (not attorney) was Magnitsky. The tax fraud involved laundering Russian money through Manhattan real estate. Browder and Magnitsky (posthumously) were charged with tax evasion in November 2012. Browder was convicted in absentia in July 2013. The whole "Magnitsky Affair" was under the direction of Yury Chaika, Russia's prosecutor general since 2006 and led to the 2012 U.S. Sergei Magnitsky Rule of Law Accountability Act that sanctioned 18 Russian officials supposedly involved in Magnitsky's persecution and death.[57]

U.S. prosecutor Preed Bharara filed the civil forfeiture case against Prevezon in SDNY in 2013. Prevezon finally settled for $6 million in May 2017, signed off on by U.S. Attorney General Jeff Sessions two days before the case was to come to trial. Why? Was Trump involved? Veselnitskaya gloated that the case was "settled on Russian terms."

Donald Trump Jr. visited Moscow for a conference in 2008 and announced optimistically Trump plans for hotels in Russia. He stated at a New York conference that "Russians make up a pretty disproportionate cross-section of a lot of our assets" and money was pouring in from Russia. Donald Trump Sr. may also have visited Russia six or more times in 2008, but business was still slow.

---

[57] The best account is Amy Knight, "The Magnitsky Affair," in the *New York Review of Books*, February 22, 2018 (Volume LXV, Number 3), 25-27.

Dmitry Rybolovlev and Miami Vice

In 2008, U.S. investment banks collapsed in a massive failure, culminating in the bankruptcy of Lehman Brothers. Oil fell below $100 a barrel on world market. The Russian stock index dropped 17 percent. Within months, the Russian market lost $1 trillion. By the end of December, $130 billion in capital had left Russia for the U.S. and Cyprus. Oligarchs were pawning yachts and selling private jets and sports teams. They were also buying real estate. Georgia and Russia were at war again.

Eurasian mobsters were also moving to South Florida and buying or renting the properties of Donald J. Trump, perhaps through the agency of fast-talking *Sergei Millian*, a Belarus-American con artist from Atlanta who headed something called the Russian-American Chamber of Commerce. Millian met Trump at a Miami racetrack in 2007 after Trump returned from another Moscow trip. Millian may also have been Christopher Steele's source for the salacious "golden showers" story in the Steele dossier. Miami was becoming the "Russian Riviera" because of the influx of oligarchs and criminals. At least 63 "Russians" (from the former Soviet Union) purchased property in seven Miami skyscrapers owned by the future president of the U.S. Russian mothers came to Miami to have their babies, future American citizens *in utero*. Members of an organized crime group from Rostov (joined in a nominal wrestling club) ended up in Trump Casa apartments. The three Trump hotels on Sunny Isles (Trump Royale, Trump Palace, and Trump International Beach Resort) were full of Russians, netting Trump 1 to 4 percent of the income from the hotels, amounting to $20-80 million after he became president. Trump was getting rich off Eurasian criminals, while his Sunny Isles properties were known as "Little Moscow."

Svyatoslav Mangushev moved to Miami in 2010 from Moscow. In Miami, he ran a water polo club of retired Russian Spetznaz (army special forces) officers linked to the Alpha group of the FSB intelligence organization. Mangushev named his shell company for his condominium, Trump Palace 4702. His friend Igor Zorin owned an additional three apartments in Trump Palace. The palace was a kind of Trump Tower South that was full of Eurasian criminal groups.

Trump sold a tear-down Florida mansion in 2008 to Russian oligarch *Dmitry Rybolovlev* for $95 million. Rybolovlev had spent 11 months in prison in 1996 for the contract murder of a business rival, *Evgeny Pantelymanov*, general director of Neftekhnik, a potash fertilizer business controlled by Russian mafia. He also gained control of Uralkali, Russia's largest producer of potassium-based fertilizer. By 2008, *Forbes* magazine reported that Rybolovlev was worth nearly $13 billion, making him among the 60 wealthiest individuals in the world, far wealthier than Trump. Russian gangsters in Miami tended to acquire mansions on Fisher Island, as did Aras Agalarov. Rybolovlev joined them, even though he had no interest in living in Florida and was in the midst of a messy and very expensive divorce. In the end, Trump made $50 million and Rybolovlev had the mansion torn down.

In 2011, Rybolovlev's daughter paid the highest price ever for a New York apartment, $88 million. Two years later, Rybolovlev himself purchased Leonardo da Vinci's painting *Salvator Mundi* for $127 million. In 2017, a Saudi crown prince acquired it for more than $400 million, the highest price ever paid for a painting. Rybolovlev also purchased Skorpios Island, once owned by the Greek billionaire Aristotle Onassis. Rybolovlev was awash in real money that Trump could well use. The challenge was getting Russian cash into Trump holdings without a money trail. One method was to purchase real estate from Trump.

Dmitry Rybolovlev provided Trump $50 million
profit for a Florida mansion neither man intended to use.

In 2010, Vladimir Putin helped bail out the Bank of Cyprus, which had $10 billion in Russian deposits. By now, Rybolovlev owned 10 percent of BOC shares. He was worth some $8 billion personally at the time. The FBI in *Operation Ghost Stories* arrested and expelled a dozen Russian spies who had lived as "The Americans" in the United States for years. In July, the paymaster and co-ordinator of the group, *Christopher Metsos*, escaped to Cyprus, was arrested, jumped bail and fled, possibly to Moscow Center. The Obama administration expelled 10 Russians from the U.S. and had them flown back to Moscow.[58]

"The Americans" were convicted of conspiracy to act as unregistered agents for a foreign government and conspiracy to commit money laundering. Similar charges were filed against Paul Manafort in 2017.

---

[58] See U.S. v. Christopher R. Metsos et. al., Southern District of New York, June 25, 2010. Metsos, a secret SVR agent, and the other Russian "Americans," were expelled shortly afterwards.

Enter Deutsche Bank

Deutsche Bank entrance at 60 Wall Street in New York

Deutsche Bank and the Bank of Cyprus had done business to-gether for years. *Viktor Vekselberg*, another billionaire Russian art col-lector and KGB crony of Putin, directed the Bank of Cyprus with the help of former Deutsche Bank chair, *Joseph Ackerman*. Ackerman and Deutsche Bank signed a cooperation agreement with Vneshnekonom-bank (VEB) in 2006. Vekselberg at one point repurchased a set of Russian church bells that had ended up in Harvard University's Low-ell House in the 1930s. Then *Wilbur Ross*, Trump's later Secretary of Commerce, succeeded Vekselberg as vice chair. In November 2011, Ross became a major investor in Navigator, a firm that chartered tankers to carry petrochemicals worldwide. Navigator in turn was linked to Sibur, a large Russian gas company owned in part by *Gen-nady Timchenko*, Putin's judo partner and longtime friend from the St. Petersburg mayor's office, and *Kirill Shamalov*, husband of Putin's younger daughter. Sibur is now under U.S. sanctions.

After bailing out the Cyprus bank, Putin and his German credi-tors at Deutsche Bank, Trump family bankers accused of making $10 billion from Russian money laundering, survived a bank crisis three years later that gave Russians a majority of shares in the bank and ownership. The older Russian Laiki Bank became defunct. Deutsche

Bank settled a $2.5 billion debt with the U.S. Department of Justice in 2015 (another $7.2 billion in 2016) over its stock-trading schemes for Russians moving money offshore, its toxic mortgages and its mirror trading in Moscow, London, and New York. For Deutsche Bank, money laundering was big business. And the Trumps were good customers. *Jared Kushner* had a $24 million line of credit. In October 2016, Deutsche Bank loaned him $285 million to help Kushner buy the old *New York Times* building.[59]

Another old KGB ally of Putin from 1980s St. Petersburg days was *Vladimir Strzhelkovsky*, a major Bank of Cyprus shareholder and former director of Norilsk Nickel, a company trading in nickel and palladium. Putin named him deputy premier for sports and physical education, then in 2000 head of the State Tourism Committee. In 2013, Strzhelkovsky took his $200 million golden parachute and became a director of the Bank of Cyprus. He retained his pension as a KGB Lieutenant Colonel. *Wilbur Ross*—now U.S. Secretary of Commerce—claims he helped force out Strzhelkovsky and other Russians to protect Bank of Cyprus operations. Ross had also brokered the sale of Trump's run-down Palm Beach mansion, Maison de L'Amitie, to Dmitry Rybolovlev.

On January 30, 2017, Deutsche Bank agreed to pay $425 million fine for money laundering operations that moved some $10 billion out of Russia by mirror trading stock (Moscow office buys in the morning; London sells in the afternoon.) The bank settled with the Justice Department for $7.2 million (the Department wanted $14 million).

Deutsche Bank rescued Trump as well as banks in Cyprus, Estonia and Latvia. Deutsche Bank had loaned Trump $1.3 billion since his fourth bankruptcy filing, when U.S. banks refused him. Khodorkovsky's attorney Robert Amsterdam stated that "one of Mr. Trump's main lenders is a bank that's been particularly close with Russians: Deutsche Bank," sanctioned in 2014 because of Russia's incursions into Ukraine. Indeed, both Deutsche Bank and the Bank of Cyprus provided crucial support to the complex machinations of Trump companies and family members worldwide.

[59] Harding, *Collusion*, 320.

The Cyprus Connection

A U.S. Department of State report alleged in 2011 that Cyprus was a place of "primary concern" for international money laundering. *Christopher Metsos*, the paymaster for Russian spies in America, operated from Cyprus and returned there in 2010 after the U.S. government expelled his spies. Two years later, the FBI's *Mike Gaeta* stated that Trump Tower Russians ran a major laundry from the building's unit 63A. Their money was ultimately laundered from Russia, Ukraine, and other locations through Cyprus banks and shell companies based in Cyprus and then ultimately here to the U.S.

The Russians helped rescue Cyprus. On March 25, 2013, the president of Cyprus signed a $13 billion bailout rescue agreement with the European Union. Cypriote banks closed their doors for a week to avoid a run on deposits. A collapse of the banking system seemed imminent. Finally, the government closed down the ailing Cyprus Popular Bank, or Laiki, and shifted its deposits to the Bank of Cyprus, that is, from the "bad bank" to the "good bank." Putin's Russia supported the bailout despite huge losses for Russian depositors, who made up nearly one-third of the total.

The Bank of Cyprus in 2014 also cut its ties with the Federal Bank of the Middle East (FBME), a bank registered in Tanzania that did 90 percent of its business in Cyprus. FBME had long experience getting illegally-gained Russian money into the New York real estate market. Recognizing FBME as a money laundry, Deutsche Bank cuts its own ties the same year.

In 2015, while Wilbur Ross was vice chair of the Bank of Cyprus, the bank sold off more than 100 businesses and banks inside Russia to *Artem Avetisyan*, a banker with close ties to Putin and Sberbank, the largest bank in Russia that had been sanctioned by both the U.S. government and the European Union.

Cyprus was thus an important node in the vast network of money laundering that had gone global. The Bank of New York settled in 2017 with the Russian Finance Ministry a $22.5 billion lawsuit based on Russian mafia *money laundering* in the 1990s.

Russia received $14 million in court costs plus a $4 billion discounted five-year loan from BONY. But the money laundromats continued to operate.

On April 3, 2016, the German newspaper *Suddeutsche Zeitung* published more than 11 million files of the "Panama Papers," documenting worldwide money laundering, offshore bank accounts, shell companies, and corruption through the Mossack Fonseca law firm in Panama City over the past 40 years.[60] Police raided the law firm offices and confiscated thousands of documents and computers. Trump's name was mentioned an estimated 3,540 times individually and in 32 offshore companies in the database. Trump claims that he often simply sells his brand name to companies he neither knows nor owns. Putin was livid at the exposure of his own wealth hidden in a myriad of fake accounts in the names of others, notably his old cellist friend from Leningrad, Sergei Roldugin, the cellist. But he continued to use his criminal contacts and networks to the advantage of the Russian state and his own kleptocracy.[61]

Trump's wealth, too, whatever it amounted to, was laundered and moved within a vast network of offshore banks and other financial institutions stretching from Moscow and Nicosia to Manhattan. The Bank of Cyprus and Deutsche Bank were only two of many banks involved in both legal and illegal transactions in the global market, including loans to the extended Trump family for its seemingly endless branding and building management projects. Most banks had blacklisted Trump since the 1990s and the collapse of his Taj Mahal Casino in Atlantic City. Like his gambling and real estate friends in Moscow, Trump continued to depend on Vladimir Putin's kleptocracy for its financial support. Precisely how this tangled web was spun may well take years to unravel.

---

[60] Bastian Obermeyer and Frederick Obermeier, *The Panama Papers. Breaking the Story of how the Rich and Powerful Hide their Money* (London: Oneworld, 2016).

[61] For a recent examination of Putin's use of oligarchs and criminals, see Mark Galeotti, "Crimintern: How the Kremlin uses Russia's Criminal Networks in Europe," European Council on Foreign Relations Policy Brief, April 2017. Galeotti worked for the FBI.

"You realize where all this is going," concluded former Trump strategist Steve Bannon regarding the Mueller investigation, "this is all about money laundering."[62]

And Mueller's team had the financial sleuths to explore the laundry.

---

[62] Wolff, *Fire and Fury*, 278.

HANDLING TRUMP

Emin Agalarov, Donald Trump and Aras Agalarov,
Moscow, November 14, 2013. (Anspress)

7. MOSCOW NIGHTS: THE AGALAROVS

Eurasian organized crime is our no. 1 priority.
—Rick Brodsky, FBI, *Miami Herald*, 2011

A lie told a thousand times becomes truth.
—Aras Agalarov

After 1980, the Azerbaijani (Azeri) mafias moved operations from Baku to Moscow and took over much of the heroin trade from the Chechens, who were soon embroiled in a war with Russia. The Azeris also engaged in *arms smuggling, fraud, money laundering, car theft, extortion, gambling, counterfeiting, prostitution* and *contract killing.* They invested heavily in real estate as a means of money laundering to conceal their assets.

Azeri real estate mogul *Aras Agalarov*, 33, grew up in Baku, studied computer engineering, sold bootleg films, and then managed trade fairs. His father was head of the KGB, then President, of Azerbaijan. Aras moved to Moscow from Baku in 1981 and, a year later, organized the Crocus Group of real estate projects. He also built golf courses and sold luxury footwear. In 2008, Aras Agalarov received the Order of Merit from the Italian government. Critics linked the Agalarov family to the mafia in Azerbaijan. By 2017, Agalarov had a net worth over $1 billion. He knew Putin personally and was a major figure in Moscow real estate business. Agalarov was also a friend of *Yury Chaika*, the prosecutor general of Russia.[63] More importantly, he was a friend of Vladimir Putin, nicknamed "Putin's Builder."

In 2012, Donald Trump Jr. delivered a paid speech to the Baltic International Bank (BIB) in Riga and met with the bank's founder, *Valerijs Belokons*, a/k/a Valeri Balkon. The bank had branches in Moscow, Riga, Ukraine, and London. Like the Bank of Cyprus, the BIB was also heavily involved in money laundering and was under criminal investigation in Kyrgyzstan. Specifically, the bank had moved $860 million in pesos for Mexican drug cartels in 2011 through Tormex, a shell company based in New Zealand. Ostensibly, the younger Trump was simply in Riga to put the Trump brand on a new concert hall, with BIB's financing, of course. That plan fell through.

Donald Trump's attempts to launch his own real estate projects in Russia were largely a failure, so he turned his attention to other areas. As early as 1987, Trump and his wife Ivana had been flown to

---

[63] On the Agalarov family and the Trumps, see Harding, *Collusion*, 233-50. Also see Menas Associates, "Donald Trump's Azeri Connection to Vladimir Putin," November 22, 2016.

Moscow to look over prospective hotel sites while the KGB considered them as possible assets. A year later, on December 7, 1988, Trump shook hands outside Trump Tower with a "Mikhail Gorbachev" that turned to be an impersonator. In 2007, Trump launched Trump Super Premium Vodka in Moscow, but the new business failed by 2009 despite Donald Trump Jr.'s oft-cited boast that "we see a lot of money pouring in from Russia."

Money came from non-Russians as well. On April 22, 2012, Trump and Georgian president *Mikhail Saakashvili* announced plans for a 47-story $110 million luxury hotel and casino at the resort town of Batumi on the Black Sea. Trump visited both Tbilisi and Batumi. Downpayment money came from *Timur Kulibayev*, son-in-law of *Nursultan Nazarbayev*, dictator of Kazakhstan and member of Gazprom board. The Kazakh BTA Bank provided loans through the Silk Road Group in a complex process of bank fraud, shell companies, and money laundering. Partners from the Silk Road Group of developers included *Giorgi Rtskhiladze*, a friend of Trump's attorney Michael Cohen, and *George Ramishvili*. But shortly after Trump's election as U.S. president, the deal was cancelled, and the land remains an empty lot.

The Trumps and Agalarovs became friendly. In June 2013, Emin Agalarov's manager, British-born *Rob Goldstone*, had dinner in Las Vegas with Emin Agalarov, Georgian-born *Irakly "Ike" Kavaladze*, and Donald Trump. Kavaladze handled accounts for Russian brokers in U.S. banks and was accused of laundering $1.4 billion for Russians in 2000. On June 18, Trump tweeted: "Do you think Putin will be going to the Miss Universe Pageant in November in Moscow? If so, will he become my new best friend?"[64]

In February 2014, Emin met Ivanka Trump in Moscow. A month later, he played in a golf tournament in Coral, Florida at a Trump golf course and was photographed with Ivanka and The Donald. Most importantly, the Agalarovs provided one degree of separation from Vladimir Putin for Trump.

In October 2013, Trump adviser *Boris Epshteyn*—a Russian émigré who came to the U.S. in 1993—held a conference in New York

[64] TTA, June 18, 2013.

titled "Invest in Moscow!" Epshteyn, 31, attended Georgetown University with Eric Trump, volunteered for the GOP v.p. candidate Sarah Palin in 2008, and worked on securities and bank finance for the law firm of Millbank, Tweed, Hadley and McCoy. Abrasive, rude, and condescending, the giant Epshteyn was arrested in January 2014 for assault in an Arizona bar-room brawl. He joined the White House PR staff in March 2017 and resigned two months later after neglecting to mention the Jews on Holocaust Remembrance Day. Investigators are seeking his testimony.

Miss Universe Does Moscow
Donald Trump owned the Miss Universe Contest jointly with NBC from 1996 to 2015. In November 2013, *Aras Agalarov*, the Russian-Azeri owner of Crocus Expo in Moscow, paid Trump $14 million for rights to host the contest, which ultimately made $12 million for the Miss Universe Organization. His Crocus Group owned numerous properties, including two Japanese restaurants in Moscow of the Nobu chain. Trump and Agalarov dined at one of them during the contest: "We talked about business," said Agalarov, "but not his business."

Trump spent several days in Moscow (accompanied by his personal bodyguard since 2005, *Keith Schlller*, an NYPD detective) and was photographed numerous times with the Agalarovs and the comely Miss Universe contestants. Aras was jovial, welcoming and charming.

The Agalarovs also had New York connections. Aras's son Emin, 34, attended school in Switzerland and Manhattan Marymount College in New York. His sister Sheila graduated from the Fashion Institute of Technology there and opened a jewelry store in New Jersey. Emin, a rock musician, was an avid fan of Trump's "reality" TV show, *The Apprentice*. He also became friendly with Donald Trump Jr. As Trump Sr. tweeted after the pageant: "Emin from Russia—a very fabulous guy."[65]

Aras Agalarov, active in the U.S. since 1996, also purchased a number of American properties: an apartment house complex of 110 units in the Bronx (2003); a house in Tenafly NJ (1992); an Englewood Cliffs NJ condominium building (2000); a Demarest NJ mansion ($3

[65] TTA, November 20, 2013.

million in 2014) and another mansion on Fisher Island in Miami Beach FL ($10.7 million in 2016). Ike Kavaladze was a frequent visitor. Emin was often resident in his father's homes, ran a commercial recording studio and was the nominal head of Crocus USA. The Agalarovs lived close to both Trump Tower and Mar-a-Lago and at some time became good friends of the Trumps.

On November 9, organized crime boss *Tokhtakhounov* was spotted in the VIP section of Trump's Miss Universe pageant in Moscow. Tokhtakhounov then disappeared. Trump later boasted that Putin called him on the phone during the pageant. More likely, Putin's representative, *Vladimir Kozhin*, property manager for the Kremlin, actually attended the event and met Trump. Music promoter Igor Krutoy was also there.

After the pageant, Trump remained optimistic about Russian projects. Asked about Vladimir Putin on the David Letterman TV show, Trump said, "He's a tough guy. I met him once."

Did he?

Trump appeared on stage in a music video with Emin Agalarov at the Moscow Ritz-Carlton Hotel that included the inevitable "You're fired!" line from *The Apprentice*. On November 11, Trump tweeted the Agalarovs: "I had a great weekend with you and your family. You have done a FANTASTIC job. TRUMP TOWER-MOSCOW is next."[66] But it wasn't.

In December 2013, Trump entertained the Agalarovs, Goldstone, and Trump's attorney Michael Cohen at dinner in Las Vegas (where Agalarov had yet another home) to discuss future projects, including a Trump Tower in Moscow. Sberbank (sanctioned) had just announced that it was loaning Aras Agalarov $1.3 billion for such projects.

In 2014, Trump partnered with *Anar Mammadov*, another Azeri realtor, to build Trump International Hotel and Tower, a 33-story hotel in Baku. Mammadov was a London-educated, 34-year-old, golf-playing playboy and son of a former transportation minister. As usual, Trump put no money of his own into the project but simply sold his brand name. The Baku project was actually owned by the Garant company, not Trump.

---

66 TTA, November 11, 2013.

Aras Agalarov purchased his Miami condominium on Fisher Island in 2016, joining Trump and Rybolovlev as part-time South Florida residents under FBI surveillance. Trump had made millions doing business with both men and other Eurasian criminals in both New York and Miami. *Alec Simchuk* ran the South Beach rackets out of Hallandale. *Igor Zorin* invested over $5 million in Trump Palace for his Spetznatz biker club friends. The FBI was well aware that the Russians were replacing Italian Mafiosi in South Florida, well established there ever since Chicago gangster Al Capone purchased his mansion on Palm Island in 1928. Trump's public comments about having nothing to do with Russia or Russians were lies, plain and simple. If Trump lied under oath to the FBI or a special prosecutor, he would be committing a federal crime. But he had not yet done so.

Trump also persisted in trying to establish a Trump Tower in Moscow. In September 2015, he opened more planning conversations with Russians. He then signed a letter of intent on October 28. In January 2016, Trump's attorney Michael Cohen emailed Dmitry Peskov, Putin's press adviser, asking for help on the project but claimed he received no response. Cohen and Felix Sater were the go-betweens for the Trump Organization and the VTB bank in Moscow (sanctioned by the U.S. in 2014 over Crimea and Ukraine) on financing the Trump Tower in Moscow deal.

By now, the Russian government was operating its own campaign against the network of Eurasian organized crime operating within Russia. In 2016, Putin's police arrested 47 thieves-in-law, prosecuted 26 of them, and deported another 10. Eurasian crime was an international challenge whose fingerprints, murders, and bank accounts appeared everywhere. Trump, by dealing with the Agalarovs, was wading into deep shark-infested waters where he barely knew how to swim.[67]

---

[67] Luke Harding, "How Trump Walked into Putin's Web," *The Guardian*, November 15, 2017.

The Famous Dinner with Putin in Moscow, December 2015.
Flynn is adjusting his hearing aid.

8. MICHAEL FLYNN, RUSSIAN AGENT

That's a total witch hunt, the whole Russia story. It's a hoax.
It's a hoax. We had no collusion with Russia. We never dealt with Russia.
—Donald J. Trump, 2017

Our boy can become president of the USA and we can engineer it.
I will get all of Putin's team to buy in on this, I will manage the process.
—Felix Sater e-mail to attorney Michael Cohen, late 2015

Vladimir Putin succeeded beyond his wildest dreams when he began
a strategic campaign to meddle in the American presidential elections
of 2016 and prevent the election of Hillary Clinton through cyberwar
and disinformation. Soviet and Russian meddling abroad had been
part of foreign policy since World War II. The U.S. also meddled
routinely in foreign elections. A key Russian agent in this latest campaign was a U.S. army general named *Michael Flynn*, who had visited
Moscow in 2013. Flynn had spoken with Russian ambassador Kislyak

in late 2016 and was then named National Security Council head by the new U.S. president, Donald J. Trump.

Michael Flynn joined the Trump campaign in February 2016 as a military and foreign policy adviser. Born and educated in Rhode Island, Flynn began his distinguished military career in 1981 with the U.S. Army. He oversaw intelligence operations in both Iraq and Afghanistan and then served for two years (July 2012 to August 2014) as the Defense Intelligence Agency's (DIA) director, a position from which President Obama removed him. Flynn was an outspoken critic of Obama's policy on Syria and Islamic terrorism. Within months, Flynn became a paid agent of the Russian government by accepting money (over $65,000) from the official news and television agency *Russia Today* and several Russian companies. He also served as an agent of the Turkish government but failed to register as either a Turkish or Russian agent as required by law (FARA).[68]

Trump's campaign for U.S. President revealed a number of his ties to Russian intelligence and Eurasian organized crime that had begun decades earlier. On July 26, 2008, Ukrainian *Sergei Kislyak*, 58, became Russian ambassador to the U.S. in Washington DC. Kislyak was trained as an engineer and worked for the Soviet/Russian Foreign Ministry since 1977. His father was KGB station chief in Paris. From 1981 to 1985 young Kislyak worked in Manhattan for the Soviet mission to the U.N. He then served as first secretary to the embassy in Washington. With his ambassador appointment, Kislyak also became the nominal overseer of Russian espionage operations in the U.S., thus under FBI surveillance. (He returned to Moscow in July 2017.) The Obama administration was well aware of these operations, having expelled a dozen Russians posing as Americans in 2010 and another 35 spies in January 2017. Trump followed up by expelling 62 Russian agents in March 2018 after Putin had a retired FSB-MI6 double agent in England poisoned with a military-grade nerve agent, Novachok.

Kislyak first met Donald Trump in April 2016 when Kislyak had a front-row seat for a Trump foreign policy address. We do not know how many times they may have met subsequently.

---

[68] On Michael Flynn, see Luke Harding, *Collusion*, 114-141.

One should remember that Putin's campaign for a third term as president in 2011 led to massive street protests across Russia. Putin later blamed Hillary Clinton, then U.S. Secretary of State, for giving the "signal" to set off the protests and meddle in the Russian election campaign. The Russians naturally continued their traditional policy of meddling in foreign elections themselves. But from the Russian viewpoint, the Americans had meddled in their elections first, and Hillary Clinton was the prime meddler. Russia was now encircled by nearly 30 NATO member nations stretching from the Baltic to the Black Sea.

Cyberwar

Putin saw disruptive opportunity well before the Trump campaign began. On April 8, 2013, three Russian intelligence agents met to discuss the possibility of recruiting *Carter Page*, a future Trump campaign adviser, as a Russian spy. Michael Flynn made his officially approved visit to the GRU headquarters in Moscow that year (the first ever visit by a foreign military officer). But Putin was especially intrigued by disinformation and cyberwar as a novel and effective strategy of conflict.

The Russian interference in the U.S. presidential campaign in 2016 was not Russia's first cyberattack. A decade earlier, on April 26, 2007, after Estonia had committed to joining NATO, Russian hackers disabled Estonian publications, medical and banking records, and the mail server for the Estonian parliament. Botnets of captured and linked computers brought down entire computer systems using automated queries. Troll farms proliferated. Hansabank had to stop all online banking services and card transactions. Then on May 19, the attacks suddenly ceased. But the Estonian trial run showed that Russian information warfare could be an effective national strategy of disruption in other countries. Russian meddling in various European elections continued for the next decade.

Putin in 2015 launched a cyberwar to disrupt the American elections.[69] From January 2015 to August 2017, the Kremlin-linked Internet

---

[69] On the 2016 cyberwar attack, see Malcolm Nance, *The Plot to Hack America. How Putin's Cyberspies and Wikileaks tried to Steal the 2016 Election* (NY: Skyhorse Publishing, 2016).

Research Agency (IRA) posted on Facebook some 80,000 online articles and advertisements regarding divisive U.S. issues—police brutality, black activism, gender discrimination, and so on. The IRA was outed as a Russian dirty tricks operation in 2014 by an employee/troll of the agency, Ludmilla Savchuk, who had turned whistle blower and was willing to talk. The Agency also posted some 3,000 accounts on Twitter in the fall of 2016, creating an army of fake online followers. The Russian news channel *Russia Today* created a large online audience by setting up fake accounts with Google's YouTube. Russian hackers invaded both State Department and White House computer systems. The Russian cyberattack carried nicknames associated with bears: Fancy Bear was GRU, military intelligence; Cozy bear was FSB, the former KGB. They followed in the paw prints of Beserk Bear, Energetic Bear, Team Bear, and Voodoo Bear.

Cozy Bear, or Advanced Persistent Threat 29 (APT 29), first broke into the Democratic Party's computer systems in December 2015. Fancy Bear, or APT 28, showed up in spring 2016. The Dutch General Intelligence and Security Service penetrated Cozy Bear computers as early as mid-2014, watched them for a year, and informed the CIA, NSA, and the State Department of the results. The State Department was able to eliminate the Cozy Bear presence from their computers by the end of 2014 and duly thanked the Dutch for their assistance by sending them cake and flowers.[70]

The Russians then penetrated Silicon Valley. A major stockholder in Facebook and Twitter was *Yuri Milner*, 55, with hundreds of millions of dollars from the Kremlin's VTB Bank and Gazprom. Milner was a Silicon Valley mogul trained in Russia as a physicist who later worked at the World Bank and ran his own venture capital firm, Digital Sky Technologies (DTS Global). Milner's backing came not only from the kremlin but from the Uzbek-Russian oligarch *Alisher Usmanov*.

Donald Trump formally announced that he was running for U.S. president on June 16, 2015. Any remarks he made about Putin and Russia were positive. In July, he noted in a Las Vegas speech that "I don't think you'd need the sanctions" imposed by the U.S. government

[70] *Washington Post,* January 26, 2018.

on Russia in the future. Trump tweeted that he had "nothing to do with Russia," and "I don't know who Putin is."[71] Such lies did little to deceive the FBI, which had dealt with Trump and his housing of Eurasian organized criminals for decades. And on May 20, 2015, Trump hosted his young Russian fan Emin Agalarov in his office in Trump Tower. The Agalarov family was closely connected to Vladimir Putin and was now friendly with Trump after the Miss Universe pageant in Moscow.

The U.S. Senate confirmed the appointment of James Comey as director of the FBI for a 10-year term on July 29, 2013. President Obama formalized the director's appointment in September, and Comey immediately became involved in monitoring Russian espionage in America. On July 10, 2015, the FBI opened *Midyear*, a criminal investigation into former Secretary of State Hilary Clinton's handling of classified information on her home server. She called it a "security review."

In late 2015, British intelligence at GCHQ Cheltenham reported SIGINT (signals intelligence) interceptions of suspicious interactions between the Trump campaign advisers (especially Carter Page) and Russian agents. The British informed John Brennan at the CIA and helped trigger the July 2016 FBI investigation of the Trump campaign well before Christopher Steele's famous dossier surfaced. Cheltenham's electronic "doughnut" building was the nerve center of British intelligence gathering through a spying alliance called "Five Eyes" that included the U.S., U.K., New Zealand, Canada, and Australia. Together they had surveillance around the world.

The Russian sports world was as corrupt as national politics. In November 2015, the World Doping Agency suspended the Russian government's Anti-Doping Center in Moscow. Despite its title, the Center was largely responsible for covering up the doping of more than 1,000 Russian atheletes since 2006 and assisting the FSB in destroying positive evidence (urine test results). The Center's director, *Grigorii Rodchenkov*, also head of the Sochi Olympics testing laboratory in 2014, admitted his longstanding complicity in the scandal and

---

[71] TTA, October 26, 2016.

became a whistleblower. In January 2016, Rodchenkov fled to the U.S. and found safety for his family in the FBI's witness protection program. As a result of his testimony, the International Olympic Committee in December 2017 banned Russia from participation on the Winter Games in Pyeonchang, South Korea.

In Like Flynn

On December 10, 2015, General Michael Flynn, now a Trump supporter, and Vladimir Putin met in Moscow. Flynn first met Trump in 2014 when Obama was removing Flynn as DIA director. Flynn was co-author with right-wing journalist and alleged Israeli and/or Italian agent, *Michael Ledeen*, a principal in the old Iran-Contra scandal, of a book that demonized Islam, Iran, and terrorism. Flynn knew virtually nothing about Russia and was a useful idiot in waiting. He signed his emails to Russians "General Misha." His son helped out with the Trump campaign and lied that Hillary Clinton was running a child pornography ring out of a Washington D.C. pizza parlor.

Ambassador Kislyak issued the invitation to Flynn. Flynn received more than $65,000 from the Russian government TV station and news agency *Russia Today* in 2015 to give speeches. As we have seen, Flynn was seated next to Putin at a tenth-anniversary dinner and photographed, along with *Sergei Ivanov*, a KGB officer first stationed in Africa, then Putin's Minister of Defense; *Mikhail Prokhorov*, owner of the Brooklyn Nets basketball team; *Viktor Vekselberg* from the Bank of Cyprus; *Jill Stein*, the Green Party candidate for U.S. president; and *Cyril Swoboda*, a highly placed official from the Czech Republic formerly in charge of STB, Czech intelligence. Despite receiving Russian payments, Flynn failed to register as a Russian foreign agent in the U.S., as required. Flynn first met Trump in 2014 after Flynn resigned from the Defense Intelligence Agency at Obama's request. Who picked up the Czech was unclear, but Putin, in a June 2017 TV interview with NBC's Megyn Kelly, naturally denied any active involvement in the dinner or the table arrangements. But both Flynn and Jill Stein were considered idiots useful to Putin in his strategy of disrupting the U.S. elections and defeating Hillary Clinton.

Michael Flynn and Donald J. Trump (CNN)

This was Flynn's second invited visit to Russia. In 2013, the GRU's director, *Igor Sergun*, paid Flynn's way to Russia as a U.S. military intelligence coordinator. GRU officers found the whole visit very strange. Flynn was erratic, unable to think logically, and seemed a bit crazy. His imaginary "Flynn facts" rarely had any basis in reality. Obama fired him in August 2014 and warned Trump before his inauguration not to re-hire Flynn, which Trump promptly did anyway. Trump and Flynn met again in August 2015, setting the stage for Flynn's December visit to Moscow. Flynn was essentially a Trump adviser on Moscow's payroll but neglected to register as a foreign agent under FARA. In September 2016, Flynn received two $11,000 payments from the Kaspersky Laboratory, a Russian cybersecurity firm banned in the U.S., and a Russian cargo airline company, Volga-Dnepr Airlines. Why?

On January 21, 2016, a British House of Commons report concluded that Vladimir Putin was essentially responsible for the 2006 murder with Polonium 210 of former KGB agent *Alexander Litvinenko* in London. The murder was well known and documented but had not been previously linked by a foreign government directly to Putin. Coming on the heels of the doping scandal and the defection of *Grigory Rodchenkov* to the U.S., the Litvinenko murder accusation reduced Putin's already low standing in American public opinion.

Then on March 6, 2016, a young and inexperienced Chicago college graduate (DePaul U., 2009) named *George Papadopolous* joined the Trump campaign as a foreign policy adviser interested in better relations with Russia. A week later, he met in Italy with a London professor of international relations linked to the Kremlin, *Josef Mifsud*. They reconvened in London to plan a possible meeting between Trump and Putin. Mifsud also informed Papadopolous that the Russians had "dirt" on Hilary Clinton, including numerous e-mails. Papadopolous continued to imagine a trip to Russia to arrange a meeting between Trump and Putin through the summer but was rebuffed by Manafort and other Trump campaign officials, while he continued his romance with his fiancée, *Simona Mangiante*, who soon believed Papadopolous was playing an important role for and with Trump.

Mifsud was a charming con artist from Malta who served at for-profit "universities" in Rome, London, and Stirling, Scotland. He had no office and was quite unknown to his supposed students. In July 2012, Mifsud resigned as president of European-Mediterranean University in Portoroz, Slovenia (home of Trump's third wife, Melania) because of unexplained expenses incurred by him. He claimed to have met both Putin and Foreign Minister Lavrov at the annual Valdai Discussion Club in Sochi. Some suspected he was a Russian "cut-out," a non-governmental intermediary for a Russian agency, perhaps the FSB.

Trump announced that Papadopolous was a member of his campaign team as a foreign policy adviser on March 21, 2016. On March 31, Papadopolous met with Trump, Jeff Sessions, and others on his campaign team. He proposed he work through his London contacts to arrange a meeting between Trump and Putin. Trump listened intently, but Sessions and others nixed the idea. Trump later feigned ignorance of both Papadopolous and the meeting, despite photographs of him at the same table.

On April 11, *Olga Polonskaia* of the Foreign Ministry responded to a Papadopolous email that "the Russian Federation would love to welcome [Trump] once his candidature [i.e. nomination] would be officially announced." By April 18, Papadopolous was in London, where his friend Professor Mifsud introduced him to *Ivan Timofeev*, a

Moscow contact with the Foreign Ministry. On April 22, Mifsud and Papadopolous skyped about a potential meeting between Russian government officials and Trump campaign agents. On April 25, Papadopolous emailed Trump adviser Stephen Miller that "the Russian government has an open invitation by Putin for Mr. Trump to meet when he is ready."

Papadopolous persisted. On May 4-5, he forwarded an email from his contact Timofeev saying that the Ministry of Foreign Affairs in Moscow was "open for cooperation" with the Trump campaign. The email went on to Corey Lewandowski and then Paul Manafort. Carter Page suggested Trump go to Moscow. Papadopolous on May 21 discussed a possible meeting with Russian state officials at a Trump campaign meeting.

The idea of a Trump-Putin meeting was in the air. In May, a National Rifle Association (NRA) enthusiast, *Paul Erickson*, emailed Rick Dearborn, a Trump campaign staffer who had worked for years for Senator Jeff Sessions. He entitled the email "Kremlin Connection." Erickson suggested that the Trump campaign might use the forthcoming NRA convention in Louisville, Kentucky, to establish "first contact" regarding a Trump-Putin meeting prior to the election. They would meet with *Alexander Torshin*, a Russian banker, NRA member, and godfather of the Taganskaia mob, wanted in Spain on money laundering charges. Taganskaia was a subsidiary of the Solntsevo mafia network in Moscow. *Alexander Malyshev* of the Tambov mafia network in St. Petersburg moved to Malaga on Spain's Costa del Sol around 2000 after living in Germany and becoming an Estonian citizen. Torshin and Malyshev laundered some €10 million through a network of hotels, markets, restaurants, and casinos using the Bank of Cyprus. They soon attracted the attention of the Spanish police, who raided Russian mafia hideouts across the country on June 13, 2008 in operation "Troika."

Donald Jr. favored the idea of his father meeting with Putin, but Jared Kushner opposed it. Erickson claimed that Putin would welcome a Trump visit to the Kremlin. Torshin later claimed he had met Trump in April 2015 at the annual NRA convention in Nashville,

Tennessee. Indeed, the NRA had a friendly organization in Moscow called the Right to Bear Arms, headed by Torshin's young protégé, *Maria Butina*. Former UN ambassador John Bolton made a video for Putina's organization in 2014 urging Russians to adopt something like the Second Amendment to the U.S. Constitution on the right to bear arms. But it is hard to imagine Putin himself having any enthusiasm for the Second Amendment in Russia, where weapons were strictly limited to the military, the police, and hunters. An armed citizenry in Russia was an unwelcome invitation to revolution.

But Trump adviser Carter Page was working along the same lines as Papadopolous to get Putin and Trump together. The fact that the Logan Act forbade American private citizens from negotiating with foreign leaders was no deterrent, since it was rarely used to prosecute anyone. But the FBI was already watching (and listening) closely.

Carter Page

In March 2016, the little-known *Carter Page* joined the Trump team as a so-called Russia expert.[72] Page, 46, a U.S. Naval Academy graduate (1993) first visited Moscow in 1991. He subsequently received an M.A. from Georgetown, an M.B.A. from NYU business school, and a Ph. D. from the University of London (he failed his oral exams twice, and his thesis supervisor, the Uzbek *Shirin Akiner*, recalled only that Page was one of his many students). He served with the U.S. Marines as an intelligence officer in the Western Sahara before becoming an energy consultant to both Merrill-Lynch and Russia's Gazprom in Moscow in 2004. Page worked for the Merrill-Lynch office in Moscow until 2007 and purchased his own shares in Gazprom while living there. Page was an outspoken supporter of Russia, Putin, and Putin's hench-man in Ukraine, Viktor Yanukovych, who lost power in 2014. Page also started his own Global Energy Capital LLC in 2008 in New York with another Gazprom executive, *Sergei Yatsenko*. (Page was Global

---

[72] On Carter Page, see Jason Zengerle, "What (if anything) Does Carter Page Know?", *The New York Times Magazine*, December 24, 2017, 26-7. See also Page's rambling testimony to the H.R. Permanent Select Committee on Intelligence, November 2, 2017 and Luke Harding, *Collusion*, 22-56.

Energy's only employee, and he rented his office.) Page's speeches and writings were unfailingly pro-Russian and flattering to Putin.

Carter Page's new company was located in the IBM Building at 590 Madison Avenue adjacent to Trump Tower and linked by a glass atrium to the Tower. The FBI monitored Page's emails in April 2013 and discovered Page was in contact with two Russian spies, *Victor Podobny* and *Igor Sporyshev*, both attached to the UN for cover. In an FBI wiretap, Podobny considered Page an "idiot." (The founder of Page's previous employer, the Eurasia Group, thought Page was a "wackadoodle.") The FBI intervewed Page in June 2013 about his meetings with the Russians. Page denied all, but the FBI had evidence Page was a Russian agent sufficient to convince a judge to let the FBI under FISA monitor Page's electronic communications, which they did. Trump went ballistic over this because of the Nunes memo (from Republican members of the House of Representatives Special Committee on Intelligence, or HRSCI) of February 2018 critical of the FBI's use of the Steele dossier in persuading the FISA judge to permit wire tapping Page (plus three 90-day renewals).[73]

But the FBI had been onto Page for three years and had other sources. By 2018, Carter Page was simply another pawn in President Trump's game of attacking the Department of Justice and the FBI in a Roy Cohn-like attempt to divert attention from the special counsel's investigation of the Trump campaign to supposed plots within the Department of Justice by Democrats to defeat Trump. He thus completely ignored the evidence beyond the Steele dossier available to the FBI, and the fact that the FBI investigation long pre-dated the appearance of Carter Page on the scene.[74] And he (and HRSCI) failed

---

[73] HRSCI Majority Members memo to staff (declassified by Trump February 2, 2018), "Foreign Intelligence Act Abuses at the Department of Justice and the FBI." The Nunes memo claims Christopher Steele received "over $160,000" from the DNC and Clinton campaign, but never names Fusion GPS or Glenn Simpson as the company that hired Steele. The memo is a generally worthless attack on DoJ and the FBI that sheds no light on what we know about the Carter Page affair.On Page's 2013-5 contacts with Russian spies, see U.S. v. Evgeny Buryakov, a/k/a "Zhenya", Igor Sporyshev, and Victor Podobny,U.S. SDNY, January 23, 2015.

[74] The January 23, 2018 HPSCI Minority Report, "Correcting the Record—The Russia Investigation," shows clearly that the FBI began investigating Carter Page

to mention that Steele was paid by Glenn Simpson and Fusion GPS, not the Democrats or the Hillary campaign.

Page was casually vetted by the Trump campaign, which signed him up in March 2016. He spoke Russian poorly and had no training in Russian studies or history. His company failed in 2008 to raise funds sufficient to invest in Turkmenistan oil and gas industries. But he remained breathtakingly loyal to Putin and the Russians. His statements on Russia could have been, and may well have been, written in Moscow.

Carter Page lectured in Moscow, July 2016,
and worked on the Trump Campaign.

Page's most powerful Russian contact was *Igor Sechin*, 56, head of Rosneft, the dominant Russian energy company and a longtime administrator for Putin since Putin worked for the mayor of Leningrad, Anatoly Sobchak, in the 1990s. Before that, Sechin also did oil exploration and military translation work in Angola and Mozambique, where he overlapped with KGB officer *Sergei Ivanov* and may have first met Carter Page. Page considered Sechin had "done more to advance U.S.-Russian relations than any individual in or out of govern-

---

years before Steele's dossier reached the FBI, which produced its first FISA request to monitor Page on October 26, 2016. FBI surveillance was renewed through September 2017 three times on 90-day warrants. Both Page and Papadopolus interacted with Russian agents.

ment from either side of the Atlantic over the past decade." Sechin was, and remains, a close friend and business associate of U.S. Secretary of State *Rex Tillerson*, former head of ExxonMobil, who negotiated expanded drilling rights for oil in the Arctic and Black Sea in 2012, later put on hold because of U.S. sanctions on Russia. Tillerson had known Putin since 1999, when his company Exxon Mobil, tried to drill for oil on Sakhalin Island. Tillerson, Putin and Sechin remained in close contact ever since.

Sechin is also the second most powerful man in Russia. Some call him "Putin's brain cells." In 2004, Putin named Sechin to be chief of Rosneft, the giant oil and natural gas company run by the Russian government. In March 2014, the U.S. government put Sechin and Rosneft on a list of sanctioned Russians with whom Americans should not do business because of Russian military aggression in Ukraine and Crimea. Rex Tillerson nevertheless signed a series of agreements with Sechin personally (not Rosneft) and thus effectively circumvented the sanctions. In July 2017, the Treasury Department's Office of Foreign Asset Control levied a trivial $2 million fine on ExxonMobil, which responded by suing the U.S. government.

Igor Sechin and Vladimir Putin presenting an award to
Rex Tillerson in February 2015.

Carter Page's main contact with Sechin was *Aleksandr Baranov*, who was in charge of investor relations for Rosneft and earlier for Gazprom. Page and Baranov got to know each other in Moscow when Page lived there (in 2004-2007). Page joined the Trump team in March 2016, signed a nondisclosure agreement with *Sam Clovis*, an Iowa talk-show host working for Trump, and talked about his upcoming trip to Moscow in July 7-8 to give a speech to the New Economic School, whose rector, *Shlomo Weber*, was also a U.S. citizen. (Journalist Luke Harding described Page's speech as a "content-free ramble verging on the bizarre.") Page's speech was broadcast by ultranationalist Alexander Dugin, a philosopher much enamoured of Hitler, Putin and Trump, on Dugin's TV station. In Moscow, Page met *Arkady Dvorkozich*, a deputy prime minister to Putin, and intelligence officer, Igor Diveykin, but denied meeting Sechin. On July 19, Chris Steele emailed Fusion GPS that Page had attended "secret Kremlin meetings" that did indeed include Sechin.

The Trump campaign, especially *J.D. Gordon*, objected to Page's trip, but Page got permission from campaign manager Corey Lewandowski anyway. Page later claimed he briefed the Trump team both before and after his Moscow visit. He returned to Moscow and London in December 2016, where he met *Sergei Yatsenko*, who introduced Page to the Kazakhstan ambassador to Great Britain.

Jared Kushner and the Meeting

The Trump-Russia connection went forward. In May 2016, Jared Kushner and the Trump campaign hired Cambridge Analytica (CA), a "global election management agency" that uses demographic, consumer behavior, and internet activity to engage in "behavioral microtargeting" of voters. CA was founded in 2013, but its British parent company SCL (founded in 2005) is run by Iranian-British entrepreneur *Vincent Tchenguiz* (b. 1956) whose Iraqi-Jewish family moved to Britain from Teheran in 1979. SCL employed a number of foreigners, including Russians like *Alexander Kogan*, to mine millions of Facebook accounts for personal information and political preferences. *Dmytro Firtash* was a major shareholder in SCL using his Cyprus company

Spadi Trading, owned by his main company Group DF. In the U.S., CA was funded by hedge-fund billionaires, *Robert and Rebecca Mercer*, who first supported Ted Cruz for president (June 2015-April 2016), then switched allegiance and money to Trump. CA successfully supported the winning Brexit vote in Britain and spent some $15 million on the Trump campaign. CA also spent millions on 44 political races in 2014. CA and Vote Leave (Brexit) both used websites and landing pages provided by AggregateIQ, a computer firm in Victoria, British Columbia, Canada.

Steve Bannon, Breitbart news journalist and future White House aide, was a Mercer-funded CA vice president and link to the Trump campaign. He appears to have been a significant contributor to Trump's election, but after a tell-all book on Bannon by Michael Wolff called *Fire and Fury* appeared in January 2018, Trump dismissed Bannon as a disgruntled ex-employee who had "lost his mind" and sued Bannon to stop publication. Robert Mueller subpoenaed Bannon to testify before a grand jury on the Trump campaign and the Russians. The fact that CA employees were mainly British and Canadian, that the CA CEO *Alexander Nix* was British, and that attorneys warned Bannon and the Mercers that they might well be liable for illegal campaign contributions of foreign money in the U.S. made future prosecution of CA likely. Indeed, in March 2018, Facebook suspended all CA operations on the Facebook platform. Nix allegedly offered to purchase Hillary Clinton's 33,000 deleted emails from Wikileaks in 2016, but Julian Assange refused. He cheerfully enjoyed Internet access from his refuge in the Ecuadorian embassy in London until the embassy cut him off in March 2018.

On March 1, 2016, two weeks after Trump clinched the Republican nomination for U.S. president, the Agalarovs wrote Trump wishing him luck in the campaign. Rob Goldstone, Emin's manager and a judge in the Miss Universe pageant in Moscow, offered to help set up a meeting with Trump campaign officials in New York. So did Emin Agalarov. On June 3, Emin telephoned Goldstone and said a Russian "crown" [British term] prosecutor (*Yury Chaikov*) had offered to provide the Trump campaign with documents that would "incriminate

Hillary and her dealings with Russia." Another e-mail described the proposed meeting as: "Russia—Clinton—private and confidential." Donald Jr. emailed Goldstone back that "if it's what you say I love it especially later in the summer." The collusion was on.

As Goldstone emailed Trump Jr. on June 3: "Emin just called and asked me to contact you with something very interesting," he wrote. "The Crown prosecutor of Russia met with his father Aras this morning and in their meeting offered to provide the Trump campaign with some official documents and information that would incriminate Hillary and her dealings with Russia and would be very useful to your father. This is obviously very high level and sensitive information but is part of Russia and its government's support for Mr. Trump—helped along by Aras and Emin."

Another inexperienced member of the Trump team, *George Papadopoulos* (an "excellent guy," proclaimed Trump) emailed seven other team members in March offering to set up a meeting with the "Russian Leadership," including Putin. Cooler heads resisted the notion, citing the Logan Act that prohibits U.S. private citizens from negotiating with foreign government officials. In May, Paul Manafort called a halt to the Papadopoulos initiative. But Papadopoulos meanwhile met the Australian delegate to the U.K., *Alexander Downer*, at an upscale London bar and told him that Moscow had "dirt" on Hillary Clinton in the form of thousands of emails from April.[75] Downer told his superiors, who dutifully informed the FBI in July.

The conspiracy bore fruit that summer. On June 9, Donald Trump Jr. met in the 25th-floor conference room of Trump Tower with Paul Manafort, Jared Kushner, Rob Goldstone, and *Natalia Veselnitskaya*, 42, Agalarov's lawyer and a Russian attorney-lobbyist in Washington against the sanctions of the Magnitsky Act (2012), including halting American adoptions of Russian children. In addition, Veselnitskaya had represented the FSB Military Unit 55002 in land acquisition court cases in 2011-2012 after defending Moscow developers (since 1999) and maintaining regular contact with prosecutor *Yury Chaika*. She was also a trusted Moscow insider who in May 2017

---

[75] BBC News, December 30, 2017.

helped *Denis Katsyv* settle money laundering charges brought against his Prevezon Co. by prosecuting attorney Preet Bharara, later fired by President Trump. We now know that Manafort took copious notes at the meeting.

In 2017, President Trump naturally denied any knowledge of the 2016 Trump Tower meeting and praised his son Donald Jr. for releasing related emails. Yet Trump, aboard Air Force One on July 8, 2017, dictated as president a possibly false statement about the meeting that suggested Trump feared the meeting might be a criminal act. Was Trump obstructing justice? Former White House adviser Steve Bannon later suggested that the meeting (in the Trump Tower conference room on the floor below Trump's apartment) was "treasonous," and that both Trump and his daughter Ivanka might probably have met the participants briefly.

Montage of the Trump Tower meeting principals: Rinat Akhmetshin, Natalia Veselnitskaya, Jared Kushner, Donald Trump Jr., and Paul Manafort (Yahoo.com)

Putin denied having ever heard of Veselnitskaya. Lies proliferated and lawyers ransacked the Federal Election Laws seeking definitions of "conspiracy" and "collusion." Putin reiterated the traditional falsehood that "Russia never interferes in the internal political processes of other states, especially the United States." Trump continued to deny any link to Putin or Russia. The two liars mirrored each other consistently.

The source of the Clinton material was apparently *Yury Chaika*, 66, the prosecutor general of Russia. Opposition leader *Aleksei Navalny* and his Anti-Corruption Foundation investigated Chaika and his links to organized crime in December 2015. "Everyone knows," Navalny concluded in his report, "that Chaika is a thief and a murderer."[76] Chaika and his sons Artem and Igor had gotten rich through the Irkutsk Oblast Prosecutor's Office in the Soviet period, then later, when Putin tapped Chaika as minister of justice, later prosecutor general, in the new Russia. Chaika was reappointed in June 2016. He was also a good friend of the Agalarovs and owned houses in Switzerland and Greece. Information thus flowed easily from Putin and Chaika through the Agalarovs to the Trump campaign.

On June 3, 2016, Chaika had dinner with Aras Agalarov and asked the Azeri businessman to arrange a meeting between the Veselitskaya circle and the Trump campaign. The resultant June 9 meeting included *Rinat Akhmetshin*, 48, a former Red Army intelligence officer, teenage friend of Trump's attorney, *Michael Cohen*, an American citizen (2009) and registered U.S. Congressional lobbyist in Washington D.C. with Veselnitskaya for their Human Rights Accountability Global Initiative Foundation, a Kremlin-funded lobbying firm. Smart and slick, Akhmetshin helped found the Eurasian Institute for Economic and Political Research during the Clinton years. Akhmetshin served in Afghanistan (1986-1988 and 1991) and entered the U.S. in 1994 to study Biochemistry at Georgetown U. In November 2015, he was accused in the New York Supreme Court of hacking the computers (28,000 files or 50 GB) of the International Mineral Resources (IMR) company in July for the Russian fertilizer and chemicals oligarch *Andrei Melinchenko* and his potassium mining company EuroChem VolgaKally.

The Russians offered "high level and sensitive information" against Hillary Clinton. Akhmetshin and Veselnitskaya both had dinner with Glenn Simpson (see below) on June 10 and later turned up at Trump's inauguration, along with Alexander Torshin's former assistant on gun-rights matters and the National Rifle Association, Maria Butina.

---

[76] Knight, "Magnitsky Affair," 25.

After the June 2016 meeting in Trump Tower, businessman *William Browder* (Hermitage Capital Management) complained to the Justice Department that Akhmetshin had not registered as a Russian agent under FARA. Browder was a well-known businessman operating between New York, London, and Moscow.[77] A British citizen, Browder was also the grandson of his namesake, the founder of the American Communist Party. Since 1990, Browder shuttled between Moscow and London, amassing some $4 billion in investment stocks for Hermitage Capital from 1996 to 2005. After Putin finished persecuting and arresting Mikhail Khodorovsky, he expelled Browder from Russia in November 2005. Browder promptly hired his accountant, *Sergei Magnitsky*, to plead his case in court. As corruption enveloped Russia, Magnitsky and Browder became noisy and dangerous threats to Putin's kleptocracy.

Sergei Magnitsky, murdered by the Russians in 2009.

After a long period of incarceration, Magnitsky was found dead in his Moscow prison cell on November 16, 2009, at the age of 37, sick, malnourished and beaten by his captors. Putin had murdered another political enemy, and in December 2012, the U.S. Congress

---

[77] On Browder and the Magnitsky Act, see William Browder, *Red Notice. A True Story of High Finance, Murder and One Man's Fight for Justice* (NY: Simon & Schuster, 2015).

passed the Magnitsky Act, naming some 60 Russians who had tormented Magnitsky, denied him his human rights and ultimately killed him. They were permanently denied entrance to the U.S. and sanctioned for their crimes.

On July 4, 2016, Franklin Foer, former editor of the *New Republic*, published an article in *Slate* magazine that laid out a Trump-Russia conspiracy: Trump's admiration for strongmen like Putin; his involvement in offshore companies and money laundering; his links to Russian and American hustlers (Arif, Sater, Page, Flynn and Manafort); the possibility that Trump was a Manchurian Candidate subject to Russian blackmail; and the chance that Trump and the Russians (perhaps Putin himself) had gotten together to hack the Democratic National Committee computers.[78]

The Hack

The 1986 Computer Fraud and Abuse Act prohibits unauthorized persons from gathering the private electronic information of others. This includes access to email accounts.

In June 2016, hackers invaded the Democratic National Committee computers in Washington D.C. DNC contractor Crowdstrike discovered that Russian military intelligence hackers known as Guccifer 2.0 did the hack. In August, Roger Stone allegedly communicated with Guccifer 2.0. An FBI FISA request to monitor Trump Tower and Trump's advisers was denied by the FISA court. On June 27, former U.S. president Bill Clinton shockingly met with A.G. Loretta Lynch on the airport tarmac in Phoenix, Arizona, when Hillary Clinton was under suspicion for misusing her own emails. Trump was livid. Conspiracy theories multiplied.

In fact, Russian intelligence had been hacking Clinton's campaign chair John Podesta's emails since March 19. The apparent coordinator of Russian cyberwar was the *Internet Research Agency* in St. Petersburg, handling Russian trolls and bots, but there were other agencies and individuals involved as well. As early as November 2014, an IRA employee traveled to Atlanta for four days to acquire false-identity com-

---

[78] Wolff, *Fire and Fury*, 99-102.

puter servers in the U.S. to support operations. And as late as March 2017, Putin's troll factory was still tweeting and emailing insults to anti-Trump U.S. Senators John McCain of Arizona and Lindsay Graham of South Carolina.

On July 5, FBI head James Comey at a news conference announced that no charges were appropriate in the case (*Midyear*, re: Hillary Clinton's server) and that the investigation was now closed. Comey confirmed that the FBI was investigating Russian meddling in the election campaigns but did not mention Trump.

On July 10, DNC employee *Seth Rich* was shot to death at 4:15 am in downtown Washington DC. Rich was the DNC's Voter Expansion Data Division head, recently promoted to work on Hillary Clinton's campaign. *Julian Assange* of Wikileaks, confined to the Ecuadoran embassy in London, alleged that Rich was the source of leaked e-mails from the DNC. Some maintain this was a Kremlin hit on Rich, whose computer was missing, but whose valuables were not. The Rich case became a fake news conspiracy sensationalized by Sean Hannity of FOX News. Trump allegedly urged FOX to publish the story. D.C. Police suspected a botched nighttime robbery. The only Trump campaign member in contact with Wikileaks was Donald Trump Jr., although some suspected that Peter Smith and comedian Randy Credico might have served as intermediaries between Assange and Roger Stone of the Trump Campaign.

On July 22, Wikileaks released the first batch of thousands of emails stolen from DNC computers. After investigation, on October 7, Homeland Security and the DNI jointly confirmed that Russians hacked the DNC computers and provided information to WikiLeaks, which had moved its hosting to Moscow.

Trump denied all: "The new joke in town is that Russia leaked the disastrous DNC emails, which should never have been written (stupid) because Putin likes me."[79] On the same day, Trump tweeted: "For the record, I have ZERO investments in Russia."[80] He ignored the fact that many Russians had investments in him.

---

[79] TTA, July 26, 2016.

[80] TTA, July 26, 2016.

On August 4, 2016, the CIA chief, *John Brennan*, telephoned his Russian counterpart *Alexander Bortnikov*, head of the FSB, and warned him that Russian meddling in the presidential election had to stop immediately. Bortnikov admitted nothing but agreed to pass the message on to Putin. Obama confronted Putin a month later at a meeting in Hangzhou, China, and, in the *Washington Post's* words, warned the Russian leader that "we knew what he was doing and [he] better stop or else." This threat had absolutely no effect on Putin.

In October, WikiLeaks released tens of thousands more emails stolen from the account of Hillary Clinton's campaign chair, John Podesta.

"I love WikiLeaks," Trump told a campaign rally three days later. But, as CIA director Mike Pompeo said in April, "it's time to call out WikiLeaks for what it really is: a non-state hostile intelligence service often abetted by state actors like Russia."

Behind WikiLeaks stood the Internet Research Agency and Russian military and civil intelligence. By November, some 50,000 Russian Twitter accounts had sent off more than two million tweets related to the U.S. presidential election.

The Nominee

In July, the Republican Party nominated celebrity real estate mogul Donald J. Trump for U.S. president. The FBI began an investigation into the activities of the Trump campaign and obtained a secret court order to monitor the activities of Carter Page under the Foreign Intelligence Survey Act (FISA). The 90-day court order was renewed several times. Allegedly Page—then working for the Trump campaign, where few knew who he was—met with the sanctioned energy king Igor Sechin in Moscow (or with their mutual friend, *Aleksandr Baranov*). Sechin may have offered Page a 19 percent ($11 billion) share in profits from the sale of the Quatar Investment Authority (offices in Trump Tower) and other oil-rich companies by Rosneft if Page, through Trump, could help lift U.S. sanctions on Russia should Trump be elected U.S. president.

Russian ambassador Kislyak conversed with Trump supporter Jeff Sessions, a Republican U.S. Senator from Alabama working for Trump's campaign. Sessions denied they discussed Trump campaign affairs, but they apparently did. Kislyak was a regular attendee at the Republican convention in July when he met Carter Page, Michael Flynn, Jared Kushner, and other members of the Trump team. When J.D. Gordon succeeded in watering down the GOP platform plank on sanctions on Russia for invading Ukraine, Page emailed him: "As for the Ukraine amendment, excellent work." Thanks to the Trump campaign, anything in the Republican platform that might anger the Russians had been removed or modified.

On July 27, 2016, Trump encouraged a foreign government to work against the United States. At a press conference, he called on "Russia, if you're listening" to "find the 30,000 emails that are missing" from Hillary Clinton's server and "share them with the FBI."[81]

Indeed, the FBI was busy tracking both candidates.

And the Russians were busy supporting Trump.

During the campaign, Dmitry Rybolovlev's personal airplane (a teal, cream, and black A319 Airbus) was photographed at airports in Las Vegas, Charlotte, and Concord, North Carolina, simultaneous with the presence of Trump's own aging 727 aircraft. Some suspected Rybolovlev was delivering money to Trump. Or perhaps meeting with Trump's attorney, Michael Cohen.

CIA director John Brennan had warned FSB chief Alexander Bortnikov not to interfere in the U.S. elections. A CIA task force began to monitor Russian interference from the White House situation room, excluding outsiders. On August 11, Brennan briefed eight Congressional leaders on the Russian cyberattack and propaganda. Over the next few months, the FBI learned that the Russians had interfered with voter registration systems in 21 states, compromising the one in Illinois.

On August 19, Paul Manafort resigned from the Trump campaign after reports surfaced that he was paid some $12.7 million by Yanukovych for Manafort's lobbying and consulting work in Ukrainian elections. Manafort on the same day created Summerbreeze LLC holding company to cover a $3.5 million loan on his new house in

---

[81] TTA, July 27, 2016.

Bridgehampton, Long Island. On September 26, another Trump adviser, Carter Page, took a leave of absence from Trump's campaign team while under continuing FBI surveillance and investigation. Also on September 8, Trump team member Senator Jeff Sessions had a third conversation with Kislyak.

The Dossier

Trump received his first classified briefing from the FBI in New York on August 17 prior to the election. The two advisers who accompanied him were New Jersey governor Chris Christie and future NSC member, General Michael Flynn. Trump only later began to get wind of a dossier about his Russia connections that could damage him.

On July 5, 2016, an FBI agent in Rome met with his colleague and former MI-6 British intelligence officer *Christopher Steele*, 52, to be briefed on Steele's work on an opposition research dossier on Trump's campaign and activities related to Russia. Steele was working for Fusion GPS, but the FBI would reimburse him for his travel expenses. (They did not.) The "dossier" would ultimately become 17 memoranda totaling 35 pages written by Steele regarding Trump and Russia from June 20 to December 13, 2016, under contract with Fusion GPS, a company hired by the DNC (and Republicans) since April and run by Steele's friend *Glenn P. Simpson*, a former *Wall St. Journal* reporter.

Most of Steele's "dossier" consisted of raw intelligence based on gossip and anonymous interviews with MI-6 Russian sources, who allegedly were unpaid. Steele guessed that half to three-quarters consisted of accurate information.[82] The FBI hinted at its own source inside the Trump campaign that confirmed Steele's findings.

Mike Gaeta and the FBI team in Rome were "shocked and horrified" by Steele's findings in July, but then moved too cautiously and

---

[82] The Trump "dossier" consists of 35-page memoranda by Steele running from June 20, 2016 to January 10, 2017, when Buzzfeed published the entire series on line. See also Harding, *Collusion*, 20-40, and Glenn Simpson's testimony before the U.S. Senate Judiciary Committee in August 2017, made public by Senator Diane Feinstein (D-Cal) in January 2018. Steele also passed to the FBI in October 2016 a similar memo written by journalist Cody Shearer that confirmed a number of Steele's stories.

secretly for Steele and Simpson. Steele then spoke with American journalists, and the dossier became public on October 31 (appropriately, Halloween). But Steele's careful documentation of a Trump-Russia conspiracy did not become sufficiently well known to affect the presidential election. The dossier only reached the Oval Office of President Obama's White House in January 2017. By then, it was unpublished but well-known in the media.

Christopher Steele of MI-6 (ABC News)

Steele first came to Moscow in 1990 as a British MI-6 agent. Steele's father, an army officer, moved his family from Aden to the Shetland Islands to Cyprus (twice). Steele left Russia in 1993 after the collapse of the Soviet Union. After being outed as a spy in 1999, he returned to London and investigated the Litvinenko murder in 2006 for the MI-6 Russia Desk. Three years later, Steele's wife died, and he retired from MI-6 to set up his own intelligence consulting firm, Orbis. He soon discovered that Russian intelligence, the FSB, had been seeking to cultivate Donald Trump since 2011, well before the Miss Universe contest in Moscow, picking up where the KGB left off.

Steele also became friendly with *Glenn Simpson*, a former journalist who in 2009 founded his own business and political intelligence company, Fusion GPS, in Washington D.C. Simpson was a Russian expert who had been tracking the gangster Semion Mogilevich for years and looking into Trump's links to American and Russian organized crime. He worked for Baker Hostetler law firm on the Prevezon Holdings money laundering case in 2014. And, like Steele, Simpson knew that Putin was a former KGB officer who never took action that was not deniable. Both Steele and Simpson were careful and experienced intelligence professionals themselves. They began work on the Trump campaign in May/June 2016.[83] Fusion GPS conducted exhaustive research and delivered 40,000 pages of documents to three Congressional committees along with oral testimony. Funding for the Trump-Russia project came initially from New York investor Paul Singer, an anti-Trump Republican, and only later, and partly, from GPS and the Clinton campaign. In August 2017, Simpson testified to the Senate Judiciary Committee in a closed hearing. Only in January 2018 did co-chair Diane Feinstein release the transcript to the public.

Simpson had also met Rinat Akhmetshin and Natalia Veselovskaya shortly before the notorious Trump Tower meeting in June 2016 but in connection with their work on the Prevezon case. He had met Carter Page, whom he considered "a zero, a lightweight."[84] He had once met Tefik Arif of Trump's SoHo project and Bayrock, an "organized crime figure from Central Asia" who had once been arrested for child prostitution.[85]

A second and narrower FBI FICA request to monitor communications on the Trump Tower server with Russian banks such as Alfa Bank was approved. But Trump continued to deny any Russian contacts: "I don't know Putin," he said in Kinston NC on October 26, "have no business whatsoever with Russia, have nothing to do with Russia."[86]

In fact, the FBI had discovered that the Trump Organization had leased a server named Obit.RU through Spectrum Health in Lititz, Pennsylvania (a company owned by the family of Education Secretary Betsy DeVos), and was communicating with Alfa Group in Moscow.

---

[83] Simpson testimony, 77.

[84] Simpson testimony, 241.

[85] Simpson testimony, 298.

[86] TTA, October 26, 2016.

A series of "pings" indicated that the link was tested continuously from May through September 2016. Alfa Group was headed by German Khan, a Ukrainian oilman from Kiev who had once made $28 billion by selling off his 50% share of Igor Sechin's Rosneft. Khan's son-in-law, Alex van der Zwaan, turned out to be a lawyer working for Paul Manafort and Rick Gates on behalf of Yanukovych and the Ukraine Ministry of Justice.

On October 28, FBI director James Comey in a letter to Congress reported no criminal activity on Hillary Clinton's server but stated that additional emails had turned up. Comey did not say the new emails may well have come from the FBI investigation of the Trump Campaign and Russia. Comey's public statements violated established Justice Department protocols and procedures. Trump, campaigning in Maine, tweeted, "this changes everything."[87] But Comey, in a second letter to Congress on November 6, affirmed that the Clinton case was now closed. The election was two days away.

The British later confirmed FBI suspicions. A May 5, 2017, NSA report on Russian hacking between August and November 2016 (leaked by a contractor) later described GRU cyberattacks on U.S. voter registration software, malicious hyperlinks infecting computers with malware, spoofed e-mails, and "spear-phishing" emails that invaded computer systems. VR Systems of Florida was one target. Putin and his propagandists naturally denied any such meddling in the U.S. election.

We know now that Trump campaign members had dozens of meetings with Russian officials in 2016. Christopher Steele concluded there was a "well developed conspiracy of cooperation" between the Trump campaign and the Russians. Such a conspiracy, as attorney Paul Fishman noted, requires in law "an agreement to do something that the law already forbids." Conspiratorial behavior looked obvious, but which laws might have been violated was still unclear. Steele also claimed that Trump attorney Michael Cohen and three team members had met secretly with Russians in Prague in late August or early September for "secret discussions with Kremlin representatives and

---

[87] TTA, October 28, 2016.

associated operators/hackers."[88] Cohen naturally denied that he had been in Prague at that time. Steele now went home to Surrey, England, to avoid the American media. Trump continued to maintain that he did not know any Russians.

Immediately after Trump's unexpected upset victory in the presidential election, President Obama warned Trump (on November 10) that Michael Flynn was a national security risk. Trump ignored the warning.

---

[88] Steele dossier, Buzzfeed, January 10, 2017, 34. One needs to remember that MI-6 and retired British intelligence officers had a record of forging documents going back to Mary Queen of Scots. Since Steele does not name any sources, it is difficult to confirm or deny any claims made in the dossier.

Putin's Dream? (by permission, Dave Granlund)

9. AN IDIOT SURROUNDED BY CLOWNS

Russia has never tried to use leverage over me. I HAVE NOTHING TO DO WITH RUSSIA—NO DEALS, NO LOANS, NO NOTHING.[89]
—Donald Trump, January 11, 2017

As the Father of a Family, I was like a head of state.
—Joseph Bonano

Obstruction of justice is a crime prohibited by law that intentionally impedes the government's search for truth under the law. Trump may well have committed this crime. Or not.

On November 8, 2016, Trump was elected U.S. president but lost the popular vote to Hillary Clinton by 3 million votes. His team cobbled together a wide range of frustrated voters, mainly whites from

---

[89] TTA, January 11, 2017, the day after Buzzfeed published the "dossier."

the center of the country resentful of the establishment, loss of jobs, and the paralysis of Congress. Trump campaigned against the establishment and was, surprisingly, elected president. After his initial shock and his wife's tears, Trump installed White Supremacists in the White House (Steve Bannon, Steven Miller, Sebastian Gorka). Trump also took office with an unprecedented five court cases open against him. The Secret Service promptly gave him the code name "Mogul." Melania Trump was "Muse." (Sons Donald Jr. and Eric soon accepted their fake nicknames of Uday and Qusay, after Saddam Hussain's sons.) Shockingly unprepared to assume office and govern, Trump was also due to face justice in the courts himself. The Brighton Beach voters were among the few in New York who went for Trump. Manhattan knew him all too well.

Jill Stein, the Green Party candidate, played a spoiler role. She received a total of 1,207,241 votes (1 percent) in the general election. More importantly, Stein's votes in Michigan, Pennsylvania, and Wisconsin, where Trump won narrowly, were larger numbers than his margin of victory in each case. Putin's confidence in Stein as a disrupter and useful idiot, whether or not she recognized the fact, was well placed. She garnered votes that could have helped Clinton and hurt Trump.

Now Trump continued his career of obstructing justice and buying his way out of court. On November 18, Trump paid $25 million to settle three RICO class-action fraud and racketeering lawsuits against Trump University that the plaintiffs declared was a fraudulent sham that had delivered "neither Trump nor a university" to registered students and simply made money off of suckers. Trump University was a scam, a con, and a racketeering fraud. The RICO case *Art Cohen v. Donald J. Trump* originated in federal court in New York with prosecutor Eric Schneiderman in 2013 and was to have been heard in San Diego by a U.S. District Court judge from Indiana whom Trump attacked as a person of Mexican origins who was therefore unfair to Trump because of Trump's obsession with building a wall along the Mexican border and his negative comments about all Mexicans. How Trump found the money to settle was, as usual, unclear.

On the same day, Citibank in Washington DC deposited $120,000 in the Russian embassy payroll account for use by Ambassador Kislyak. And the Kremlin may well have let Trump know that former presidential candidate Mitt Romney, hostile to Putin's Russia, would not be nearly as qualified a candidate for the next U.S. Secretary of State as Rex Tillerson, longtime friend of both Putin and Igor Sechin of Rosneft.

From the Russian standpoint, Putin and his surrogates had successfully installed their candidate in the White House after bankrolling his campaign and rescuing him from bankruptcy. The Russian Duma members stood and applauded when they received news of Trump's election. Large cardboard photos of Trump and Putin decorated Moscow bars. No wonder. Now what?

Back Channels

In November/December, Trump aides, including Michael Flynn, conducted telephone conversations with Russian Ambassador Kislyak. Flynn phoned Kislyak at least five times on December 29, the same day that President Obama imposed further sanctions on Russia for meddling in the U.S. presidential campaign and elections. Flynn telephoned Mar-a-Lago and probably got a go-ahead from Trump, *K.T. McFarland* of the NSC, or Jared Kushner. Flynn and Kislyak discussed sanctions and a pending UN resolution regarding settlements in Israel. Jared Kushner wanted to block the resolution. Jeff Sessions spoke several times with Kislyak. Kushner explored with Kislyak a secure and encrypted back channel between Trump and Putin that would be free of any government scrutiny. (The Kennedys put such a back channel to Khrushchev to good use during the Cuban missile crisis of October 1962.)

Also in November, Trump met with Preet Bharara and asked him to stay on as attorney general for the SDNY. He would soon fire him.

The Russian contacts continued. On December 12, Trump's son-in-law Jared Kushner and his assistant, *Avi Berkowitz*, met with *Sergei Gorkov*, head of Russian government's Vnesheconombank (Foreign Economics Bank, or VEB) on whose board Putin sat. (As Prime Minister, Putin had been bank chair in 2008-2012.) VEB was wholly owned by the Russian government and was sanctioned in 2014 by the U.S. over Ukraine, along with VTB and Sberbank. The VEB office in Manhattan served as a center for Russian espionage. Gorkov graduated from the FSB academy in 1994 and worked for Sberbank under *Herman Gref*, who organized Trump's Moscow meeting with "oligarchs" in 2013. The Toronto hotel financing goes back to a 2004 meeting between Trump and *Alexander Shnaider*, the Russian-Canadian steel tycoon whose Zaporizhstal company owned a smelting plant in Ukraine in which VEB held shares. Russian ambassador Kislyak set up the Kushner-Gorkov meeting and also met with Flynn and Kushner at Trump Tower. Carter Page visited Moscow for a few days around December 8. On December 26, *Oleg Erovinkin*, a KGB/FSB officer close to both Putin and Igor Sechin who may have been a source for Christopher Steele's dossier, was found dead in the trunk of his car in Moscow. The Russians claimed a heart attack; others suspected murder.

But the truth was slowly emerging. On December 19, economist James S. Henry published an article in *The American Interest* on Trump's private Russian and Eurasian connections with a "far-flung network of outright mobsters, oligarchs, fraudsters, and kleptocrats."[90] Henry was among the first to point out that Trump had longstanding ties to Eurasian organized crime that went back decades to the occupants of Trump Tower. Trump hardly needed direct connections to Putin's government in order to achieve Russian funding and influence peddling for his own purposes.

Forbes magazine estimated that the wealthiest Russian oligarchs had made $29 billion collectively out of Trump's election. Their campaign cost very little. Financially, the Russians profitted from the U.S. election, and at very little cost.

Sanctions

The Obama administration then imposed new sanctions on Russia on December 29 for meddling in the U.S. presidential elections and ex-

---

[90] Henry, James S. "The Curious World of Donald Trump's Private Russian Connections," *The American Interest*, Vol. 12, No. 4 (December 19, 2016).

pelled 35 Russian officials from the U.S. The next day, December 30, Putin announced he would not retaliate for U.S. sanctions just imposed by Obama administration. Trump tweeted: "Great move on delay (by V. Putin)—I always knew he was very smart."[91]

The Trump-Ukraine connections resurfaced. In January 2017, Felix Sater, Trump's attorney Michael Cohen, Dmytro Firtash and Paul Manafort conveyed a "peace plan" for Ukraine by *Andrii Artemenko* to the White House via Michael Flynn. Cohen convened the group in the Loews Regency Hotel in New York to work out the details of the plan. Cohen's wife was Ukrainian and his father-in-law owned an ethanol company in Ukraine. The plan (documents in a brown paper package) involved a 50-year Russian lease on Crimea and eastern Ukraine in return for lifting U.S. sanctions. The current Ukrainian government immediately rejected the plan, and the mysterious package of documents disappeared.

American intelligence agreed on Russian perfidy. On January 6, 2017, the CIA, FBI, NSA, and DNI reported unanimously that Vladimir Putin had personally directed Russian cyberattacks and a broad propaganda campaign intended to defeat Hillary Clinton and elect Donald Trump. "Vladimir Putin ordered an influence campaign in 2016 aimed at the U.S. presidential elections," DNI James Clapper told the Senate intelligence committee, continuing that the Russian campaign went far beyond computer hacking and included disinformation, propaganda, and fake news. Trump naturally denied any such campaign happened or any involvement if it did.

On January 10, *Buzzfeed* published online the 35-page "dossier" on Trump prepared by retired MI-6 Russian expert Christopher Steele. The dossier indicated that the KGB/FSB had *kompromat*, compromising salacious material on Trump's personal behavior in Moscow that was suitable for blackmail. Senator John McCain showed the dossier to FBI director James Comey. Comey flew to New York and briefed Trump on the Steele dossier at Trump Tower. Other U.S. intelligence officials briefed both President Obama and President-elect Trump on the document. Trump angrily dismissed the Steele dossier

---

[91] TTA, December 30, 2017.

as "fake news" that was "unverifiable."[92] *Buzzfeed* was a "failing pile of garbage" and a "left-wing blog." Carter Page referred endlessly to "the dodgy dossier" in his incoherent testimony before Congressional committees. Putin's press spokeman, Dmitry Peskov, called the dossier a "complete fake," not "worth the paper it was written on."

But the dossier was in fact a carefully worded series of 17 brief intelligence memos by Steele beginning in June 2016. The FBI believed in Steele's professionalism and the dossier's authenticity. James Comey began taking notes on his own conversations with Trump, assuming that the president-elect would tell lies or useful fictions about their content. He did.

Around January 11, 2017, *Erik Prince*, the pro-Trump founder of the Blackwater security firm and brother of Education Secretary *Betsy De Vos*, organized a meeting at the Four Seasons Resort in the Seychelles Islands in the Indian Ocean. The United Arab Emirates' (UAE) crown prince Sheikh Mohamed bin Zayed el-Nahyan, of Abu Dhabi, hoped a Trump-Putin back channel would help ally Russia and the U.S. against Iran. Prince was also a billionaire donor to Breitbart media and Steve Bannon of the White House staff. *George Nader*, a Washington DC Lebanese-American middleman to Zayed and the UAE was at the Seychelles meeting. So was *Kirill Dmitriev*, a Putin crony and head of the sanctioned Russian Direct Investment Fund. Whether or not this Trump-Prince Putin-Dmtriev back channel was the same as that discussed by Kislyak and Kushner in December was unclear. Nor do we know if it went into effect, or if any money-transfer or sanction-lifting commitments were made. Also at the Seychelles meeting was Kazakh *Alexander Mashkevich*, formerly Trump's partner with Felix Sater at Bayrock and Trump SoHo.

The UAE, it turns out, had received over $434 million from a Russian money-laundering scheme in 2011-2014, one of 96 countries involved in helping Russian oligarchs launder $21 billion to get their ill-gotten gains out of Russia and into profitable global investments through the banking system. Eleven of the shell companies named in the 2014 Moldovan criminal case were registered in the UAE.

[92] TTA, January 10, 2017.

Obstructing Justice for Michael Flynn

On January 15, vice president *Michael Pence* stated in public that Michael Flynn did not discuss sanctions with ambassador Kislyak. But Flynn lied to Pence, and Pence probably knew it. Did Trump?

Finally, the unexpected Trump era began. Trump was inaugurated U.S. president on January 20 with minimal crowds in the streets and maximum crowds protesting the following day. On January 22, Michael Flynn was sworn in as NSC appointee, despite warnings about him from President Obama. Two days later, the FBI interviewed Flynn at the White House. When Putin made his first hour-long phone call of congratulations to Trump, Michael Flynn sat in on the Oval Office telephone conversation. Flynn hung on as NSC head until February 13, when Trump forced him to resign. Flynn's NSC term was the shortest on record.

The following day Trump asked James Comey to stay behind after an Oval Office meeting and told him: "I hope you can see your way clear to letting this go, to letting Flynn go." Comey was wisely silent.

Trump had plenty of warnings about Flynn that he ignored. On January 26, acting AG *Sally Yates*, 56, alerted White House Counsel *Don McGahn* that Flynn had lied to Pence about discussing sanctions with Kislyak. She also warned McGahn that as NSC head Flynn would be subject to Russian blackmail. Yates arrived at DoJ as deputy to Loretta Lynch and was a threat to Trump because of her extensive knowledge of white-collar fraud and political corruption, especially emanating from New York.

Trump tried personal pressure. On January 27, he invited FBI director Comey to the White House for dinner. Comey was shocked to find himself the only guest. Trump told him "I expect loyalty," but Comey exhibited only a stunned silence in the face of a U.S. president acting like a mafia godfather.

On January 28, Trump and Putin spoke by telephone for an hour. Two days later, Trump fired acting AG Sally Yates, allegedly for refusing to defend Trump's executive-order travel bans on selected Muslim countries, more likely to weaken the Russia investigations now under way.

Trump then belatedly turned on Flynn. Trump had fired Flynn from NSC partly for lying to Pence about his sanctions conversations with Kislyak—17 days after Yates warned the White House that Flynn was a security risk. The next day Trump cleared the room except for Comey and told him regarding the Flynn investigation to "let this go." On February 15, another suspected Russian agent, Carter Page, denied meeting any Russian intelligence officers in 2016. On March 9, Flynn registered belatedly as a foreign agent of Turkey, not Russia, in the U.S., as legally required.

On November 30, 2017, General Michael Flynn pled guilty in a D.C. federal district court to making "materially false, fictitious and fraudulent statements" to the FBI about his December 29, 2016, conversations with ambassador Kislyak regarding lifting U.S. sanctions against Russia and delaying a vote on a pending UN Security Council resolution regarding Israeli settlements. And Flynn had failed to register as a Russian agent. But Trump tweeted on December 3: "I never asked Comey to stop investigating Flynn."[93]

Firing Comey

James Comey arrived at Trump Tower on January 6, 2017, to brief the incoming president on the FBI investigation of Russian meddling in the campaign. He also laid out the claims in the Steele dossier that Trump had cavorted with prostitutes in Moscow in 2013. A few weeks later, after Trump's inauguration, Trump dined alone with Comey at the White House, asked him if he wished to keep his job and added, with regard to the Russia investigation, "I need loyalty, I expect loyalty."

Comey was shocked, but noncommital.

In February, Trump cancelled a meeting scheduled with *Alexander Torshin*, deputy governor of the Bank of Russia, NRA enthusiast, and an ally of Vladimir Putin. The Spanish police were then investigating Torshin for his links to Eurasian organized crime, especially the Taganskaia syndicate in Moscow. (Torshin operated from the Costa del Sol in Spain.) The White House wisely found something else for

[93] TTA, December 3, 2017.

Trump to do, rather than meet with a Russian criminal in the oval office. Trump tweeted that "Russia talk is FAKE NEWS put out by the Dems and played up by the media, in order to mask the big election defeat and the illegal leaks."[94]

Trump now used Stalin's chilling phrase "enemy of the people" to describe the media.[95]

On March 4, Trump absurdly tweeted that President Obama had wiretapped Trump Tower. This lie obscured the historical fact that the FBI had routinely tapped tenants in Trump Tower since 1980 because of criminal investigations into Trump business associates and Eurasian organized crime. Trump's tweet reflected the politics of lying, denial, accusation and misdirection that he learned well decades ago from Roy Cohn. And Trump may well have cooperated with the FBI wiretapping himself.

Angered by Trump's endless tweets, Comey asked DoJ officials to refute Trump's lies, but got no action. Comey confirmed the FBI investigation into Russian meddling, but on March 30, Trump telephoned Comey and asked him to "lift the cloud" over his administration by stating publicly that he, Trump, was not personally under investigation. Trump reiterated this request in another phone call on April 11 asking Comey once again to "get the facts out" regarding Trump's supposed non-investigation.

On March 10, Roger Stone admitted to exchanging August 2016 messages with Russian hackers known as Guccifer 2.0. Later, on March 31, Stone said, "I've had no contact with Russians." Analysts believed Guccifer was simply another code name for the GRU and FSB hacking operations known as "Cozy Bear" and "Fancy Bear."

On March 11, Trump fired Preet Bharara as New York federal prosecuting attorney after he refused the customary request to resign.[96] Bharara immediately transferred his substantial files on Trump

---

[94] TTA, February 26, 2017.

[95] Andrew Higgins, "Trump Embraces 'Enemy of the People', a Phrase with a Fraught History," *NYTimes*, February 26, 2017. Stalin borrowed the phrase from an Ibsen play and used it in his murderous purges.

[96] On Bharara's firing, see the *New York Times,* March 12, 2017.

to New York Attorney General Eric Schneiderman, who was in the process of bringing RICO racketeering charges against Trump and associates at the state level. Bharara became a distinguished scholar in residence at NYU law school. Both Bharara and Schneiderman were a threat to Trump as prosecutors who had substantial knowledge of his crimes and litigations in New York going back decades.

The pressure on Trump increased. On March 22, AG Jeff Sessions recused himself from the FBI's Trump-Russia investigation because of Sessions' prior conversations with Kislyak. Trump later attacked Sessions for his recusal and tweeted that he would never have appointed Sessions if he had known in advance of his recusal. On March 31, Trump settled (for $25 million) the lawsuit against Trump University for *mail and wire fraud, breech of contract, false advertising,* and *racketeering.* Again, Trump utilized borrowed money to escape criminal charges.

On March 28, the White House reportedly tried to block Sally Yates from testifying to the House intelligence committee, another attempt to obstruct justice.

The Russia story would not die. In April, Rex Tillerson, U.S. Secretary of State, met with Putin in Moscow. But the U.S. Treasury Department rejected ExxonMobil's request to lift sanctions on drilling in the Black Sea (not the Arctic). ExxonMobil had filed a drilling request with Rosneft in 2015. Paul Manafort declared that he would now register in the U.S. as a foreign agent of Russia because of his work for Yanukovych. *Richard Dearlove,* former head of MI-6, stated that Trump borrowed money from Russia and Russians in 2008 during the financial crisis. Dearlove alleged that Trump's relationship with Russia went back many decades. He also admitted British SIGINT intercepted at Cheltenham had picked up Trump-related signals traffic in 2015 involving Russia. The British had indeed alerted U.S. intelligence about Trump.

On May 8, Sally Yates testified before the Senate intelligence committee. Trump tweeted: "The Russia-Trump collusion story is a total hoax, when will this taxpayer funded charade end."[97]

---

[97] TTA, May 8, 2017.

Not soon, it would seem. New York Attorney General *Eric Schneiderman* now issued a state, not federal, indictment of Trump under RICO involving the Bonanno family and Russian mafia underlings tied to Felix Sater. In fact, the FBI had arrested 10 men in New York on RICO charges in late March. The net was tightening.

Trump went ballistic. On May 9, Trump fired FBI director James Comey, who only learned about his firing on TV during a trip to California. The official letter of termination was allegedly drafted by Rod Rosenstein, deputy to AG Jeff Sessions, and signed by Trump. (In fact, White House aide *Stephen Miller* probably wrote the initial draft.) On the same day, the Senate intelligence committee requested that the Criminal Investigation Division of the Treasury Department turn over all financial information related to Trump, his top appointed officials, and Trump campaign aides. Trump promptly and repeatedly claimed that Comey had told him on three separate occasions that he was not under investigation. Some believed Trump was taping their conversations, but no one knew for sure.

On May 10, Trump met at the White House with Russian foreign minister *Sergei Lavrov* and ambassador Sergei Kislyak. Russians took photos and released them to the public. Trump allegedly provided classified information to the Russians about terrorist plans to use laptop computers on airplanes. The White House issued denials that any classified information was released, and later argued that the president had the right to discuss the same information. However, the top-secret information came from Israel, a U.S. ally, and was not Trump's to declassify. Trump admitted the Israeli source while on a trip to Israel in April, denying only that he had ever used the word "Israel" in the conversation.

Trump in passing referred to recently fired FBI director James Comey as "crazy, a real nut job." Putin offered to provide Trump with a transcript of the meeting if he needed one. The Russian photographer, *Alexander Shcherbak*, recorded everything, while the U.S. press was entirely excluded from the meeting. But for FOX news correspondent Liz Trotta, the problem was not Comey but Trump: "He's an idiot, obviously," Trotta said.[98]

---

[98] Wolff, *Fire and Fury*, 223.

To which Trump's friend Tom Barrack later added: "He's not only crazy, he's stupid."[99]

Secretary of State Rex Tillerson outdid that one at a Pentagon meeting on July 20, 2017, when Tillerson called Trump a "moron."[100]

Lavrov, Trump, and Kislyak, May 10, 2017, in the Oval Office. Transcript available only in Moscow. (Alexander Shcherbak/TASS)

Meanwhile AG Jeff Sessions recused himself from the Russia investigation, which became more serious after on May 17 acting AG Rod J. Rosenstein appointed *Robert J. Mueller*, former FBI director, the new special prosecutor. Mueller's job was to conduct a "full and thorough investigation" of Russian interference in the 2016 election campaign. By the start of 2018, Mueller's investigation was in full swing, indictments had been handed down, and the Trump White House was busy denying everything and whining about living under a "cloud" of suspicion. The staff was in disarray, a backbiting collection of ill-prepared incompetents who never thought their boss would win the election.

Finally, James Comey was able to tell his side of the story to the Senate Select Committee on Intelligence on June 8. He calmly informed the American people via television that the U.S. president was

---

[99] Ibid., 233.

[100] According to NBC news reporter Stephanie Ruhle, her source told her that Tillerson actually called Trump a "fucking moron." MSNBC, October 4, 2017.

a liar who could not be trusted and who might well have tried to obstruct justice by his pressure on the FBI director who knew too much. Trump himself admitted that he fired Comey because of his investigation into Russian meddling in the U.S. election. Trump's attorney Marc Kasowitz promptly labeled Comey a "leaker."

During a June 11 TV interview on *This Week*, Preet Bharara claimed the Comey statements were "absolutely evidence" that an obstruction of justice case could be brought against Trump for firing Comey. Robert Mueller, the special counsel appointed by Rod Rosenstein at the Justice Department without consulting Trump, continued to pursue his own investigation independent of Congress and the White House. Trump asked White House counsel Don McGahn to fire Mueller, but McGahn refused and threatened to resign.

The Witch Hunt

Also in June, the FBI, assisted by the ICE (immigration/customs enforcement) and the NYPD arrested 32 members of an extended Eurasian immigrant crime family, run by thief–in–law *Razhden Shulaya*, 40. Shulaya Enterprise was based in New York and operated in Atlantic City, Miami, and Philadelphia. Shulaya himself lived in Edgewater, New Jersey, and was arrested in Las Vegas. He arrived in the U.S. in 2014 as a Georgian from St. Petersburg and built an empire of theft, drug smuggling, and reprogramming casino gambling machines. His gang consisted of 15 Georgians plus another 17 Russians, Jews, Ukrainians, Armenians, and Kyrghyz. He and his gang were indicted under RICO as a "racketeering conspiracy."

The geography of the Shulaya Enterprise closely resembled that of Trump's own homes, hotels, and organizations. The FBI was on target. But Shulaya did not live in the White House.

The Odd Couple, July 2017, Hamburg, G-20 Summit.

On July 7, 2017, Trump and Putin met face to face in Hamburg, Germany, while both attended the G-20 summit there. There were two private meetings, presumably both recorded by the Russians. "I strongly pressed President Putin twice about Russian meddling in our elections," tweeted Trump; "he vehemently denied it."[101]

Trump spent the rest of the year railing against the "witch hunt" closing in on him, evoking the language of Roy Cohn and Joseph McCarthy. He hinted that the U.S. would return the two Russian mansions in the U.S. that Obama had seized in partial retaliation for election meddling. He praised Donald Jr. for his "transparent" admission of Russian collusion in June 2016, much of which the president himself dictated on Air Force One on his way back from Germany, claiming the Trump Tower meeting was about adopting Russian children, not getting the dirt on Hillary Clinton. Trump was engaged in lying while possibly attempting to obstruct justice by wittingly creating a false document.

Trump also urged his recused Attorney General, Jeff Sessions, to resign and tweeted insults about Sessions daily. He tried to compare Russia's involvement with the Trump campaign with Ukrainian involvement with the Hilary Clinton campaign. He tweeted daily on the forth-

---

[101] TTA, July 9, 2017.

coming testimony of Jared Kushner and Paul Manafort before the U.S. Senate Intelligence Committee. And he protested as unconstitutional the overwhelming Congressional vote in August for a bill to levy more sanctions on Russia and to prevent Trump from lifting them. Trump signed the bill. The Countering America's Adversaries through Sanctions Act (CAATSA) required the president to sign a list of Russian politicians and businessmen who were, or might in the future be, under sanctions. The January 2018 list included 210 names (including Sechin but not Putin), of which 96 were so-called "oligarchs." The list was simply a copy from a *Forbes* magazine article. Trump hinted he had no intention of enforcing sanctions imposed by Congress. Publishing a dated open-source list was Trump's joke on Congress.

The net was tightening. Trump had his own White House team of Manhattan lawyers at taxpayer expense, exploring whether or not he had presidential power to pardon himself. His team included Ty Cobb, John Dowd, and Jay Sekulow. Sekulow, from Long Island, had been general counsel for *Jews for Jesus* since 1986. Numerous investigators were looking into impeachment procedures and constitutional law issues.

Meanwhile, nearly unanimous Congressional sanctions on Russia (which Trump was compelled to sign on August 2) led Moscow to expel some eight hundred U.S. diplomats and staff from Russia. Senate, House, and Justice Department investigations went forward. Most were Russian nationals, not U.S. citizens. The U.S. responded by closing the San Francisco consulate, a well-known espionage center since before World War I. The Trump White House remained chaotic and faction-ridden until another ex-Marine, *John Kelly*, replaced Reince Priebus as chief of staff and fired another obnoxious and obscene communications director imported from Manhattan who lasted two weeks on the job. Robert Mueller called for two grand juries, and Congress considered measures to keep Trump from firing Mueller and to maintain the investigation if he did.

On August 18, 2017, in the wake of Nazi and Klan violent demonstrations in Charlottesville, Virginia, Trump fired his White House adviser *Steve Bannon*, who left office claiming that the Trump presidency was now over and returned to his right-wing media company, Breitbart. *Sebastian Gorka*, a British-born Hungarian-American of white nationalist leanings, was forced out a few days later. But the Russia question persisted and so did Robert Mueller as the noose tightened around Trump and his associates—Michael Flynn, Paul Manafort, Donald Trump Jr., and Jared Kushner.

Trump did not fire alt-right and Breitbart spokesman *Richard Spencer*, whose Russian wife, *Nina Kouprianova*, was the U.S. translator and promoter for *Alexander Dugin*. Dugin was an unofficial ideologue for Putin, arguing that Russia was a Eurasian country superior to the decadent Atlantic West, who made a neo-Nazi film about Hitler in 1993 and proclaimed Crimea and Eastern Ukraine to be part of "Greater Russia" when Putin gobbled them up in 2014.[102] Dugin brought Putinism into the White House.

In late October 2017, Mueller produced his first indictments regarding the Trump campaign of 2016. A campaign volunteer, George Papadopolous, pleaded guilty on October 5 to the crime of lying to the FBI, with whom he had been working since January and cooperating since his unpublicized arrest at Dulles Airport on July 27. Paul Manafort turned himself into the FBI and pleaded not guilty to laundering more than $18 million (of $75 million) through overseas shell companies in Cyprus, Seychelles, and St. Vincent, and Grenadines, plus conspiring against the U.S. government. Manafort's aide, *Rick Gates*, also surrendered to the FBI and pleaded not guilty to laundering another $3 million, plus similar crimes.

Charges against Manafort and Gates included conspiracy to launder money, conspiracy against the U.S. government, failing to register as foreign agents under FARA, making "false, misleading, and fraudulent" statements, and failing to file required reports on their foreign bank accounts. Then, on November 30 came the two-page indictment of General Michael Flynn for lying to the FBI about his pre-inauguration conversations with Ambassador Kislyak.[103] Flynn pleaded guilty and continued to talk with investigators. Flynn had "flipped" on

---

[102] Masha Gessen, *The Future is History,* 236, 482.

[103] U.S. v. Michael Flynn, U.S. District Court, District of Columbia, Nov. 30, 2017.

Trump. He was singing like a bird, and Trump knew it.

As yet another distraction, Trump declared Jerusalem to be the capital of Israel, with the U.S. embassy to be moved there from Tel Aviv. He thus reversed the actions (if not the words) of every U.S. president since the founding of Israel in 1948. Curiously, Putin issued his own Russian statement in April, seven months before Trump, recognizing West Jerusalem as the capital of Israel and East Jerusalem as the capital of any future Palestine. After Trump's declaration, the Russians stated only that they were concerned that the U.S. announcement could aggravate the Israel-Palestine conflict. But once again, Putin's prior support of Trump injected another note of chaos into American affairs. And the UN General Assembly overwhelmingly rejected Trump's decision on Jerusalem.

By the end of Trump's first year in office, he could boast of only one single legislative initiative, a tax reform bill that passed Congress just before Christmas. True enough, many Republican initiatives, such as eliminating the Obama mandate for all Americans to carry health insurance, were buried inside the tax reform bill. The rest of Trump's actions were executive orders, many of them tied up in the courts awaiting final judgement. And the "cloud" of Robert Mueller's special investigation into the Trump campaign's collusion, or conspiracy, with Russia still hung heavy over the White House. Indictments against Trump White House staff were multiplying. Talk of firing Mueller had given way to talk of Mueller's ability to threaten Trump and his White House with numerous revelations of criminal activity and grounds for impeachment. Trump might call Steele's dossier a "crooked Hillary pile of garbage."[104] But he could not escape its stench.

Trump and the Republicans now began to attack the FBI and Justice Department as politically aligned against Trump (like two thirds of the country). As Trump prepared for his first State of the Union address, in January 2018, FBI deputy director Andrew McCabe took early (by two months) retirement as Trump savaged McCabe and his family for being active Democrats. Trump naturally denied forcing

---

[104] TTA, December 26, 2017.

McCabe out. Would Rod Rosenstein be next? Many thought so.

If Trump tried to fire Mueller again, as he had attempted in June 2017, Mueller's team would unleash a firestorm of indictments against Trump, and he knew it. Many of these would essentially dismantle the global house of cards that made up Trump's financial empire without having to go through the messy process of impeachment. Mueller made sure Trump knew that blackmail worked both ways. The Trump brand was at risk. Trump was a cornered Russian asset and therefore extremely dangerous, but also extremely vulnerable. Even Congress was considering passing legislation forbidding Trump from firing Mueller as special prosecutor.

The Trump Family in Power (ABC News)

10. ORGANIZED CRIME FAMILY:
MOSCOW ON THE POTOMAC.[105]

The beauty of me is that I'm very rich.
One of the key problems today is that politics is such a
disgrace. Good people don't go into government.
—Donald J. Trump

If this is true, it's treason.
Vice President Joe Biden, January 2017

In November 2016, Vladimir Putin succeeded beyond his wildest dreams and helped install a useful Russian asset, Donald J. Trump, in the White House. A Eurasian kleptocrat and friend of Russian oligarchs was now President of the United States. Chaos and division followed, precisely as Putin had hoped and schemed. Congress remained in gridlock, unable even to fund the government in January 2018. The justice system was eroded by resignations, firings and the appointment of less competent, if not incompetent, judges. The FBI and Department of Justice were suspect and soon under attack by Trump. Income inequality rose, along with Wall St. market indices.

---

[105] This title relates to a much earlier article on Russian culture in Washington DC from thirty years ago: L. Peat O'Neil, "Moscow on the Potomac," *Washington Post*, September 25, 1987.

Both main political parties seemed locked in civil war. Voting fraud and election results were cited without evidence. Public information essential to a democracy, and any criticism of Trump, became "fake news." Citizens were rightly skeptical of all news reports.

The Republic was in danger, and Putin had installed a regime sympathetic to Russia (he thought) without firing a shot. Igor Sechin's friend Rex Tillerson was Secretary of State. The Bank of Cyprus financier Wilbur Ross was Secretary of Commerce. The CIA director, Mike Pompeo, met in the U.S. with his Russian FSB counterpart, Sergei Naryshkin, on the U.S. sanctions list since 2014 because of the Russian seizure of Crimea and parts of Ukraine. (Pompeo was later nominated to succeed Tillerson as Secretary of State.) The Trump family was in the White House. The new theaters of war were in cyberspace and in media disinformation. And Russia had won a major victory. Supposedly, the United States was deeply divided: red v. blue states, male v. female, black v. white, immigrants v. natives, and so on. And the Russians exacerbated every division it could find.

Donald Trump is the most litigious and litigated U.S. president in history. By 2016, he had faced more than 3,000 federal and state court cases against him and his companies, 100 of which he settled to avoid trials and possible prison sentences. He was complicit in many crimes but has never gone to jail himself. He either let others take the fall or settled—with borrowed money—to avoid being brought to justice. Nor had he ever held a real job in his life.

For the narcissistic Trump, improving his brand by making money was the whole point of life. Indeed, the purpose of campaigning for the presidency and then governing the country was to enrich Trump and his family and to improve the Trump brand. Unexpectedly, Trump won the election. How much he will profit by his election victory and time in office remains to be seen.

Donald J. Trump and his family have been under Soviet, Russian, and Czech surveillance ever since Trump married Ivana Zelnickova, a Czech citizen, in 1977. What connections or contacts Ivana Trump might have had with Czech intelligence officers remain unknown, but her entry into the U.S. followed the established Canadian pattern for

STB agents and assets. By 1985, the Trump-Zelnickova family was on file with both Czech intelligence and the Soviet KGB, hence in files available to the young Dresden intelligence officer, Vladimir Putin.

Trump has done business with U.S., Russian, and Eurasian organized crime families ever since the building of Trump Tower began in 1980 with the aid of illegal and underpaid Polish workers and the cement of Tony Salerno. The Tower and Trump Taj Mahal in Atlantic City New Jersey were favorite residences and watering holes for Russian and Eurasian mobsters, as well as American mafia leaders and Chinese bankers. So were Trump hotels in Miami and South Florida. For wealthy Russians with ill-gotten gains, Trump properties were a safe haven, an investment opportunity and a pleasure dome. That was the Trump brand.

The FBI has engaged in wiretapping and other surveillance of Trump Tower residents suspected of organized crime, with Trump's cooperation, for many decades. In April 2013, federal prosecutor Preet Bharara organized an interagency raid on the Tower and arrested many Eurasian ciminals complicit in illegal gambling. We do not know for certain whether Trump ever signed any formal cooperation agreement as an FBI informant or witness or not. If he did so, it could help explain his many narrow escapes from justice over the years.

Trump's family attorney and political mentor, Roy Cohn, had longstanding ties to both the FBI and organized crime in New York. Cohn and his gay partner, David Shine, came to prominence during the Army-McCarthy hearings of 1954. Many of Cohn's clients were Cosa Nostra figures, especially from the Genovese and Gambino families. Trump feted Cohn in a "farewell dinner" at Mar a Lago shortly before Cohn died of AIDS in 1986. Trump himself had dealings with the Gambino and Genovese crime families before turning to the Russians for financial support in the 90s.

In addition, Trump had business dealings with David Bogatin, Vyacheslav Ivankov, Semion Mogilevich, and Felix Sater, all major figures in Russian and Eurasian organized crime who rented space and conducted operations out of Trump Tower. He may also have cooperated with the FBI in monitoring their illegal activities, along with his cooperation at Atlantic City casinos, thus acquiring witness protection immunities from prosecution.

Felix Sater, whose father ran the Russian mafia in Brooklyn and reported to crime boss Semion Mogilevich, worked with Trump for more than a decade through Bayrock, a company structured to hide consumer fraud and money laundering operations for Trump. Sater inspired the Trump campaign and then in 2017 also helped arrange a Ukrainian "peace plan" given to NSC official General Michael Flynn, that went nowhere. U.S. Attorney General Loretta Lynch for a time protected Felix Sater from prosecution for stock swindling and fraud when, as a New York district attorney, she arranged Sater's signed cooperation agreements with both the FBI and CIA as an informant against international terrorists and arms dealers. In public legal documents, Sater was simply "John Doe."

Trump has a longstanding reputation for settling criminal cases against him at the last minute using borrowed money. Trump settled the Bayrock fraud case against his TrumpSoHo building project in 2011 for an estimated $4 million and the Trump University case under RICO in December 2016 for $25 million. The records in these cases were sealed and the settlement terms secret. How convenient.

How much money Trump owes which Russian and Eurasian businessmen and criminals remains unclear. We know that Trump escaped bankruptcy after 1990 through profitable business dealings with Eurasian organized criminals linked to Vladimir Putin's kleptocratic Russian government in Moscow. For example, in 2008, Trump obtained $95 million from wealthy oligarch Dmitry Rybolovlev, a Russian ex-convict once jailed for murder in Moscow, for a tear-down mansion in Florida. Trump made a profit of some $50 million. The real estate deal was an ideal way for the donor to get money to Trump rather than lose funds in a messy divorce case. Rybolovlev apparently also delivered money to Trump for his presidential campaign in 2016 by private airplane.

Trump obtained $14 million from the Agalarov family for his Miss Universe contest in Moscow in 2013. Agalarov is allegedly linked to both Italian and Azeri mafias and owns mansions in New Jersey,

Las Vegas, Switzerland and Miami. The Agalarovs also arranged the June 2016 Trump Tower meeting of Russian agents with Jared Kushner, Donald Trump Jr. and Paul Manafort, promising to deliver incriminating material on candidate Hillary Clinton from Russian prosecutor Yury Chaika.

Trump's net worth, at any rate, was miniscule in comparison with the $200 billion in offshore accounts and real estate held by Vladimir Putin and his surrogates.

Trump obtained crucial funding for his Toronto hotel from a (sanctioned) Russian bank VEB, on whose board Putin sat, after a meeting arranged by Russian ambassador Sergei Kislyak put Jared Kushner together with Sergei Gorkov, a former FSB officer and CEO of the Russian bank. Kislyak provided a crucial channel between the Trumps and Vladimir Putin until he left Washington for Moscow in July 2017.

Trump has lied repeatedly about any ties he might have to Russian and Eurasian organized crime, the Russians, Putin, or the FBI. He is literally unbelievable. His statements are simply lies intended to deceive, misdirect, or cover up his actions. They have no value for the historian except as examples of disinformation or clues to his own inner demons. The real answers lie in Trump's tax returns, bank accounts (especially Deutsche Bank), FBI files, and the visitor logs of Trump Tower, Mar a Lago, the White House, and various Trump golf courses. The money trail appears long and winding, not to mention hidden and deceptive. But it will lead to the bottom of the Trump financial swamp.

In the meantime, we must simply admire the way in which Vladimir Putin, the Russian state, and Eurasian organized crime, emerging from the ruins of the former Soviet Union after 1991, succeeded in paving Donald J. Trump's path to the White House. The cost-effective strategy of disinformation and cyberwar worked. Long before the Trump campaign conspired with the Russians, Putin's Eurasian kleptocracy had become a major player in American crony capitalism and international finance. Now the "useful idiots" and assets were occupying the White House, the Cabinet and other executive positions.

The full story of Donald J. Trump and the Russians since 1977 may not be fully known for years, if ever. Robert Mueller's final reports on the Trump campaign will be only the first steps in a long and challenging journey of historical investigation, an argument without end concerning one of the greatest presidential scandals in U.S. history. In the meantime, will the U.S. remain a democratic republic or continue to take on the trappings of a mafia state, crony capitalism, and kleptocracy that already surround us? Only time will tell.

AFTERWORD

After more than a year in office, Donald J. Trump and his family remain useful assets in Vladimir Putin's campaign to meddle in the presidential election of 2016 and disrupt American civil, legal, and cultural life. Putin has succeeded in making himself extremely wealthy and enabling his fellow oligarchs to enrich their families through the corrupt Russian kleptocracy that has replaced Soviet dictatorship. But his cyberwar and disinformation campaign against the U.S. was relatively cost-free.

Trump increasingly behaves like an authoritarian ruler, applauding himself throughout his State of the Union address (a la Khrushchev and Castro), making admiring comments about Russia and Putin, and failing to enforce sanctions levied by Congress against Russian individuals and agencies. He uses Stalin's phrase "enemy of the people" to characterize the media and the press. He imagines a gigantic military parade reminiscent of Red Square and Bastille Day that would celebrate himself. He regularly insults critics, congressmen and investigators. He remains a narcissistic businessman obsessed with maintaining his global brand worldwide and fearful that his presidency may somehow be illegitimate, hence his continuing attacks on a former president, Barak Obama, and his defeated rival, Hillary Clinton, who won the 2016 popular vote by three million votes but lost the election in the electoral college.

The cloud of Russian conspiracy with the Trump campaign still hangs heavy over a president threatened by numerous investigations. Several Trump collaborators have now been indicted by a special counsel for failing to register as Russian agents, money laundering, and lying to the FBI. Trump continues to undermine the rule of law and the Constitution by attacking his own Department of Justice, the FBI, and the very investigations closing in on him. He swore to protect and defend the Constitution but seems much more concerned with getting loyalty oaths from government employees to himself personally. "Where is my Roy Cohn?" Trump complains, thinking that the U.S. attorney general is simply another crooked lawyer who can fix things for him.

The Russian campaign became indisputable on February 16, 2018, when special counsel Robert Mueller indicted 13 Russians and their Internet Research Agency in St. Petersburg. Mueller charged that since 2014 the Russians had conspired to defraud the U.S. by interfering in its "political and electoral processes" in Project Lakhta. The 37-page indictment noted that "the conspiracy had as its object impairing, obstructing and defeating the lawful government functions of the U.S. by dishonest means," using online social media sites and fake identities.[106] The Kremlin ran the conspiracy with *Evgeny Prigozhin*, a friend of Putin since the 1990s and former hotdog vendor who made millions with a chain of restaurants and cooking schools. Prigozhin was known as "Putin's chef" and helped finance secret ununiformed Russian mercenaries fighting in Crimea and Ukraine in 2014 and in Syria in 2018 as Group Wagner, a private military company, for which he has been sanctioned by the U.S. The more than 1,000 paid writers and bloggers at the Agency were known as the "trolls from Olgino" [a St. Petersburg neighborhood] or "kremlebots."

Trump responded with a tweetstorm from Mar-a-Lago claiming that Mueller's indictment cleared him of any "collusion" with the Russians, that the Obama administration was at fault, and that the FBI was to blame for a deadly school shooting in Florida because the Bureau was too busy with the Russia investigation to stop the shooter in advance. Trump's despicable tirade had become the new normal. Hope Hicks, Trump's long-time communications director at the White House, resigned and went home. Trump was later buoyed by the House Intelligence Committee Republicans who concluded (prematurely, said

---

[106] U.S. District Court for the District of Columbia, U.S.A. v. Internet Research Agency et. al., Criminal No. 18 USC 2,371,1349,1028A, p. 10.

the Democrats) that the Trump campaign had not colluded with the Russians in the 2016 election. The Russian embassy applauded; the Democrats cried foul.

In fact, Mueller followed up a few days later by arraigning attorney Alex van der Zwaan before the court in Washington DC for making false statements about the 2012 trial of Yulia Tymoshenko while working for Manafort and Yanukovych, a felony. Mueller also filed a second round of indictments against Gates and Manafort. Then came the February 27 demotion of Jared Kushner's security clearance from "Interim Top Secret" to "Interim Secret". His final clearance languished at the FBI, probably for good reason.

Mueller also compelled a guilty plea from a California man, Richard Pinedo, 28, a computer wizard who ran an online auction site that offered methods to evade the security of digital payment accounts. Pinedo "unwittingly" sold stolen accounts to Russians who used the site; he then pled guilty to computer fraud._

Trump continues to support Putin like his banker or puppet-master. On March 13, 2018, Trump fired Rex Tillerson as Secretary of State (by tweet) after Tillerson joined Britain in blaming the Kremlin for poisoning another Russian spy and his daughter who were living in England. Prime Minister Teresa May expelled 23 Russian diplomats who were known intelligence agents. Trump was silent, then belatedly expelled 60 Russians from the U.S.

When Trump fired the FBI's Andrew McCabe two days before McCabe's scheduled retirement, he opened up a new avenue of self-destruction. McCabe worked for a decade in Manhattan as an FBI street agent and supervisor assigned to monitor Russian and Eurasian organized crime. He knows the story of Trump and Felix Sater all too well and is in a position to talk and write about mafia doings in New York. He now appears highly motivated to do so.

After Trump was elected president, Russian oligarch *Viktor Vekselberg* resurfaced in 2017, along with his American cousin, *Andrew Intrater*. Both attended (and helped pay for) Trump's inauguration. Vekselberg, at one time head of Tyumen Oil and worth some thirteen billion dollars, had also purchased nine Faberge Imperial eggs from American collector Malcolm Forbes in 2004 for around $100 million and returned them to his private museum in Moscow. By then, Vekselberg owned a $5-million home in Weston, Connecticut, and a luxury apartment in Manhattan. He remains another Russian oligarch with both Trump and Putin connections, his financial contributions laundered through Trump's Russian-born fixer and taxi entrepreneur *Michael Cohen's* shell companies.

Vekselberg donated $250,000 to the Trump inauguration fund, then another $500,000 to Essential Consultants, a shell company for Intrater's Columbus Nova LLC., with no employees, trustees or staff. He also remained head of his own Renova Management AG. Allegedly some $130,000 of Vekselberg's money went to buy silence from Trump's mistress, ex-porn star Stormy Daniels over their 2006 affair. But this mattered little. Vekselberg was one of many contributors to Trump via Cohen's slush fund. All of these transactions were engineered by Michael Cohen for Donald J. Trump. They became a subject of great interest to special prosecutor Robert Mueller and the media, especially after federal and state authorities raided Cohen's home and offices in April 2018. Vekselberg and Cohen had discussed Russian-American relations in Cohen's Trump Tower office a few days prior to Trump's inauguration. Now Vekselberg was among many Russian, Ukrainian and Kazakh oligarchs and criminals contributing to a massive money-laundering operation for Trump run by Michael Cohen in the tradition of Felix Sater and TrumpSoHo.

In May 2018, Trump further attempted to obstruct the Mueller Russia investigation by claiming that an FBI informant (Cambridge University retired professor Stefan Halper) had been assigned as a "spy" to his campaign in 2016 for political purposes. Despite no evidence of such motive or infiltration, Trump in a tweet "demanded" that the Department of Justice investigate. He threatened again to fire his attorney general, Jeff Sessions. The risk was that investigators might well discover that both Felix Sater and Trump had worked as FBI informants themselves over the years. Trump pardoned celebrity friends for past crimes. Mueller's team simply labored on without comment. And continuing FBI cooperation with Trump's investigation demands trolled him into ever more dangerous waters of obstructing justice, even as his lawyers argued in a January 2018 letter to Mueller that Trump as chief executive could not obstruct justice, was above the law and could pardon himself if necessary.

Equally important, Trump continues to oversee a vast empire of Trump-branded hotel properties around the world that he manages but does not own. His name is ubiquitous. His brand is well known to Eurasian criminals as a safe haven, a good investment, luxury accommodations and opportunities for gambling and prostitution. And this business empire and its income matter much more to Trump than being president of a government he despises and being sworn to defend a Constitution he ignores.

Any special counsel investigating Russian ties to the Trump White House and the campaign that got them there will need to ask relevant questions:

Was Donald J. Trump, like Felix Sater, protected by Loretta Lynch and federal prosecutors as an FBI informant?

How much money did Trump receive from Russian and Eurasian companies or banks after his 1990s bankruptcy proceedings? How much does he currently owe Putin's kleptocracy?

Did money flow to the Trump campaign from Russia through the National Rifle Association? How much?

What relationship did Paul Manafort have with Russian, Ukrainian and/or Italian mobsters in New York and Connecticutt?

Was Manafort an unregistered foreign agent of Russia in the U.S.? Was Trump? Same for Carter Page and Michael Flynn?

What was Wilbur Ross's involvement with Russian investors in the Bank of Cyprus?

What was Rex Tillerson's relationship with Igor Sechin and Vladimir Putin before he became U.S. Secretary of State?

What business did Trump shell companies in Cyprus actually conduct? What was Trump's financial relationship with Putin through the shell companies, banks, and agents of Russian and Eurasian organized crime? Through Deutsche Bank? The Bank of Cyprus?

Who lived in Trump Tower or other properties and belonged to the Mar-a-Lago Club? Was Trump harboring fugitives from justice?

Are the Trumps essentially another Eurasian organized crime family based in Manhattan, Atlantic City, Miami, and now Washington D.C.? Are they a clan in Vladimir Putin's international kleptocracy?

Is Trump obstructing justice by firing the director of the FBI, interfering in the Russia investigation of Robert Mueller and attacking the Department of Justice?

Was Vladimir Putin behind Cambridge Analytica's campaigns for Brexit in Britain and Trump in the U.S. presidential election? Was he behind Julian Assange and Wikileaks' release of documents related to the Trump campaign?

The special counsel may or may not be able to answer all these questions. He may have many others that he can answer. But in the long term, only historians many years from now will be able to wade through the evidence, ignore the lies and fake news, follow the money trail, and make sense of America's greatest constitutional crisis since Watergate.

Journalist Seth Hettena's investigative reporting in his book *Trump/Russia. A Definitive History* (2018) confirmed that Trump's dealings with the Russian mafia and Eurasian organized crime went back to the 1980s, that Trump Tower and other Trump properties worldwide became, after the collapse of the Soviet Union, a kind of safety deposit box where Russian oligarchs and criminals could safeguard their assets in hotels and condominiums, where no questions were asked and where substantial fortunes could be protected and increased to promote Trump's own brand and profit. Moreover, Eurasian criminals remained at the heart of Trump's business operations and money laundering. Christopher Steele's dossier seemed plausible if not provable. Trump's behavior has verged on fraud, money laundering, treason and obstruction of justice. His Russian business partners have been involved in money laundering, drugs, prostitution, arms deals, bootlegging and racketeering. The Russian active measures campaign to influence the 2016 election in Trump's favor is now undeniable. Robert Mueller has indicted a number of Russian individuals and corporations involved. Cyberwar and disinformation are ongoing. No history is ever definitive, but Hettena's book is a significant contribution to the argument without end about how Donald J. Trump and the Russians assaulted American democracy and managed from the White House a global empire of Russian-financed real estate and dark money for profit.

Saturday Night Live brilliantly spoofed Trump, Michael Cohen, Rudy Giuliani and Eric Trump eating dinner together as the Sopranos in a restaurant scene in May 2018. The actor playing Robert Mueller walked by them and said nothing. But his hand gesture suggested that he saw through the foursome, and knew things, many things, about what the mob was up to. But in Trump's mad, mad world, the only truth lies in what he believes to be the case at the present moment. In Trumpland, no evidence is allowed to challenge the belief of the moment. History, truth, democracy and the rule of law are now beyond the interests of Trump, as they always have been. They simply don't matter.

APPENDIX:
BAYROCK GROUP LLC WITH TRUMP SUBSIDIARIES

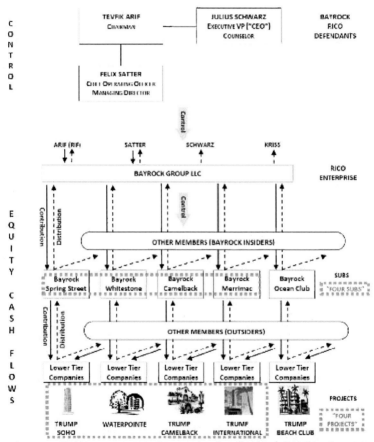

Projects are owned by lower tier companies. Outsiders are members of, contribute to, and get distributions from project lower tier companies. Bayrock's interests in lower tier companies are held in Subs, basically "special purpose Outsiders" conducting Bayrock's money in and out of projects. Bayrock Insider Sub members are usually service providers who in return for services received compensatory membership interests entitling them to distributions, so typically do not contribute cash.

BIBLIOGRAPHY

Images: All images are from Wikimedia Commons, exept as credited to other sources.

Bagli, Charles V. "Real Estate Executive with Hand in Trump Projects Rose from Tangled Past," *New York Times*, Dec. 17, 2007.

Baker, Russ, Collins, C., Larsen, Jonathan. "Why FBI Can't Tell All on Trump, Russia." *Whowhatwhy.org 2017/03/27*

Barrett, Wayne. *Trump. The Greatest Show on Earth. The Deals, the Downfall, the Reinvention.* (NY: Regan Arts,2016; first edition, 1992)

Bonano, Joseph. *A Man of Honor. The Autobiography of Joseph Bonano.* (NY: Simon & Schuster, 1983)

Browder, Bill. *Red Notice. A True Story of High Finance, Murder and One Man's Fight for Justice.* (NY: Simon & Schuster, 2015)

Davidson, Adam. "Trump's Business of Corruption," *New Yorker*, August 21, 2017.

Dawisha, Karen. *Putin's Kleptocracy. Who Owns Russia?* (NY: Simon & Schuster, 2014)

FBI, Department of Justice, "Semion Mogilevich Organization, Eurasian Organized Crime," Washington DC, August 1998.

Foer, Franklin. "The Plot against America. Paul Manafort and the Fall of Washington," *The Atlantic*, March 2018.

Friedman, Robert I. *Red Mafiya. How the Russian Mob has Invaded America* (Boston, NY, London: Little, Brown & Co., 2000)

Galeotti, Mark. "Crimintern: How the Kremlin uses Russia's Criminal Networks in Europe," *European Council on Foreign Relations Policy Brief*, April 2017.

Graff, Garret M. *The Threat Matrix. Inside Robert Mueller's FBI* (NY: Little, Brown and Company, 2011)

Gessen, Masha. *The Man without a Face. The Unlikely Rise of Vladimir Putin* (NY: Penguin, 2014)

Gessen, Masha. *The Future is History. How Totalitarianism Reclaimed Russia* (NY: Riverhead Books, 2017)

Glenny, Misha. *McMafia. A Journal through the Global Criminal Underworld* (NY: Random House, 2008)

Glushakow, H.B. *'Mafia' Don. Donald Trump's 40 Years of Mob Ties* (NY: CreateSpace, 2016)

Harding, Luke. "How Trump Walked into Putin's Web," *The Guardian*, November 15, 2017.

Harding, Luke. *Collusion. Secret Meetings, Dirty Money, and how Russia helped Donald Trump Win*. NY: Vintage Books, 2017.

Harper, Steven. "A Timeline: Russia and President Trump." *Billmoyers.com*, April 2017.

Henry, James S. "The Curious World of Donald Trump's Private Russian Connections," *The American Interest*, Vol. 12, No. 4 (December 19, 2016).

Hoffman, Nicholas von. *Citizen Cohn. The Life and Times of Roy Cohn.* (NY: Doubleday, 1988)

Isikoff, Michael, and Corn, David. *Russian Roulette. The Inside Story of Putin's War on America and the Election of Donald Trump* (NY: Hachette Book Group, 2018)

Johnson, David Cay. *The Making of Donald Trump* (NY: Melville House, 2016)

Kessler, Ronald. *The Secrets of the FBI.* (NY: Random House, 2011)

Knight, Amy. "The Magnitsky Affair," *New York Review of Books*, February 22, 2018 (Volume LXV, Number 3), 25-27.

Kristoff, Nicholas. "President Trump, if You're Innocent, why Act So Guilty," *NY Times*, February 9, 2018.

Lauria, Salvatore (as told to David S. Barry). *The Scorpion and the Frog. High Times and High Crimes* (Beverley Hills: New Millennium Press, 2003)

Lourie, Richard. *Putin. His Downfall and Russia's Coming Crash* (NY:

St. Martin's Press, 2017)

Mayer, Jane. "The Man Behind the Dossier. How Christopher Steele compiled his secret report on Trump's ties to Russia, *The New Yorker*, March 12, 2018, 48-65.

McCallion, Kenneth F. *The Essential Guide to Donald Trump.* (NY: Bryant Park Press, 2016)

Menas Associates, "Donald Trump's Azeri Connection to Vladimir Putin." November 22, 2016.

Myers, Stephen Lee. *The New Tsar. The Rise and Reign of Vladimir Putin* (NY: Vintage, 2016)

Obermayer, Bastian, and Obermaier, Frederik. *The Panama Papers. Breaking the Story of how the Rich and Powerful hide their Money.* (London: Oneworld, 2016)

Riebling, Mark. *Wedge. The Secret War between the FBI and CIA.* (NY: Alfred Knopf, 1994)

Ross, B., and Mosk, M. "Russian Mafia Boss Still at large after FBI Wiretapping at Trump Tower." *ABC News*, March 21, 2007.

Toobin, Jeffrey. "The Miss Universe Contest," *The New Yorker*, February 26, 2018, 34-41. _

Unger, Craig. "Trump's Russian Laundromat," *The New Republic*, July 2017.

Wise, David. *Spy. The inside Story of How the FBI's Robert Hanssen betrayed America.* (NY: Random House, 2002)

Wolff, Michael. *Fire and Fury. Inside the Trump White House* (NY: Henry Holt & Co., 2018)

Young, Kevin. *Bunk. The Rise of Hoaxes, Humbug, Plagiarists, Phonies, Post-Facts, and Fake News* (Minneapolis: Graywolf Press, 2017)

Zengerle, Jason. "What (if anything) Does Carter Page Know?", *The New York Times Magazine*, December 24, 2017, 24-7.

ARCHIVES AND LEGAL CASES.

Department of Justice, *Justice News*, April 2, 2014 (on Dmytro Firtash).

Donald Trump v. Timothy O'Brien and Time-Warner, New Jersey Superior Court, Case CAM-L-545-06, Trump deposition of December

19, 2007.

En.CrimeRussia.com, on line archive.

FBI file SAC (137-22152), 9/22/81, Damon T. Taylor to Daniel Sullivan (NY18904-OC).

House of Representative Special Committee on Intelligence (HRSCI), Majority Members to Staff (declassified by Trump February 2, 2018), *Foreign Intelligence Act Abuses at the Department of Justice and the FBI*, January 18, 2018.

HRSCI Minority Report, "Status of the Russian Investigation," March 13, 2018.

Kriss et. al. v. Bayrock Group LLC et. al., Southern District of NY, 1:13-cv-03905.

Kriss v. Bayrock Group, LLC, U.S. District Court, Southern District of NY, No. 10 civ. 3959 (LGS)(FM), February 1, 2016.

Page, Carter. *Testimony of Carter Page*, before the U.S. House of Representatives Permanent Select Committee on Intelligence, November 2, 1017.

State of N.Y. v. Bayrock, case index 1010478, filed under seal.

Steele "Dossier" = Christopher Steele, "U.S. Presidential Election: Republican Candidate Donald Trump's Activities in Russia and Compromising Relationship with the Kremlin," June 20, 2016, the first of seventeen intelligence memoranda published by *Buzzfeed* on January 10, 2017. Steele was a retired MI-6 agent posted to Moscow in the 1990s.

TTA = TrumpTwitterArchive.com. Searchable data base of all tweets sent from @realDonaldTrump with date and time sent.

U.S. v. Christopher R. Metsos et. al., Southern District of New York, June 25, 2010.

U.S. v. Alex van der Zwaan, Case 1:18-cr-0031, filed 02/16/18.

U.S. Court of Appeals for the Second Circuit, Case 11-479, Document 115 02/09/2018, *Felix Sater Criminal Docket—Trump SoHo—unsealing order 10-2905.*

U.S. v. Evgeny Buryakov, a/k/a "Zhenya," Igor Sporyshev, and Victor Podobny, U.S. Southern District of New York, January 23, 2015.

U.S. v. Michael Flynn, U.S. District Court, District of Columbia, Nov. 30, 2017.

U.S. v. Felix Sater, Criminal Docket No. 98 CR 1101 (ILG).

U.S. v. Internet Research Agency et. al., U.S. District Court for the District of Columbia, Criminal No. 18 USC 2,371,1349, 1028A

U.S. v. Prevezon Holdings LTD, et. al. (SDNY No. 13—CIV—6326). 88n

U.S. Senate Judiciary Committee, *Interview of: Glenn S. Simpson, Tuesday, August 22, 2017*, 312 pages. Washington DC, 2018.